I Dare to Stop the Wind

Challenging children in the
public schools through the arts & poetry

Bettina Rotenberg

Vala Book Press

Berkeley, California

i

I Dare to Stop the Wind

Challenging children in the public schools
through the arts & poetry

ISBN-13 (pbk) 978-0-615-33610-7

Vala Book Press

1605 Berkeley Way, Berkeley, California 94703

www.valaproject.org

Copy Editor

Susan Klee

Book and Cover Designer

Lee Lüng

Table of Contents

Acknowledgments

I am thankful to the following foundations for providing funding for VALA in West Contra Costa: the East Bay Community Foundation, which has supported VALA's presence in West Contra Costa from the outset; the Trio Foundation, which supported our work in the preschools in WCC from the earliest programs to the present; the San Francisco Foundation, which funded our elementary school projects this year and our preschool project two years ago; and the Lowell Berry and the Bill Graham Foundations.

I want to express my appreciation to two principals, Sonja Neely-Johnson and Susan Berrington, who dramatically increased the support for VALA artists at their schools in San Pablo and Richmond this year.

I am most grateful to my father for insisting that I write this book and following its progress page by page. I am also thankful for every VALA artist who figures in these pages and outside them, as well as for a marvelous board of advisors.

Finally, I want to thank the children who inspired me every day I came to work with them for their openness and their brilliance.

for my father

Preface

In the spring of 2006, I visited the class of a musician I'd hired to teach a kindergarten class at a school in Richmond, California. I watched the children struggle valiantly to sing and play instruments against a very nervous teacher who kept trying to get them to be quieter. It would have been actually hilarious if it hadn't been so sad — the teacher being so nervous because of the "No Child Left Behind" act which made the kids, even K kids, test constantly in reading, writing, and arithmetic, so the teacher was terribly fearful they'd fail because she'd lose her job if they did. Horrible no-win situation. I'd received emails from this teacher who was so eager to get a VALA artist, and then, poor soul, got someone who actually got her kids (Latino) to sing in English and play instruments which upset her when I was there, thinking I would share her concern about making too much noise. I laughed when I saw the kids actually enjoying themselves, raising their voices when they sang (instead of somehow – how? – singing quietly) and getting off on playing, really playing. She kept telling me they weren't usually this "wild", usually they "played by the rules" (what rules are those? Especially in a class meant to be making sound?). If it hadn't been so funny, I'd have cried. I felt like a rebel just observing these kids having so much fun. The girls, except for one little kid in pigtails, who hung out with the boys, sat there silent and sad.

One music class a week for six weeks, and no recess. That's all they got.

I've written this book for the teachers and kids I've encountered in the East Bay who are confronted by this limiting of the creative potential of children in our schools and to recount some attempts by artists in Visual Arts/Language Arts to challenge and free these children to express themselves through the arts and poetry.

1
A thrust of belief

Visual Arts/Language Arts has come to derive more meaning from its acronym, VALA, than from the composite words of its name. The visual arts did not predominate among the artists I first hired. Theater artists and musicians arrived before painters and ceramicists. The term "language arts," derived from school verbiage, is misleading. VALA artists eventually worked with districts' literacy curricula. But they combined the literary arts with their artistic disciplines, not the flat, empty prose classroom teachers drilled their students to read and write. And Vala is a character in William Blake's visionary poems, and means "tearing aside the veil that hides creativity."

The veil that conceals creativity is not endemic to the minds of the children we teach. What blocks their creative expression is the education system put in place by wrong-minded legislators and shortsighted educators. But if these children have absorbed some inhibitions to doing creative work, even "Vala" is not an accurate metaphor for how we need to teach them.

No "tearing aside" is necessary for bringing low-income minority children to the arts. More like a thrust of belief towards their innate capacities. This expectation reaches them, almost without exception. Not an easy task though, even for artists disciplined to uncover ways of challenging themselves to create.

VALA was not the first name for this organization. I founded **Kids Museum Art & Writing Project** (KMAWP) in 1995. My first step was to apply to the Tides Foundation, a fiscal sponsor, which adopts projects that "show promise of social change." A precondition for "adoption" was writing a ten-page paper. When KMAWP was accepted, I felt gratified, imagining that I was well on my way. I spent the next year submitting proposals for $25,000 to various foundations and corporations, and ended up with exactly one thousand dollars.

Discouraged and nonplused, I signed up for a two-day fundraising class. I reported my year of failed attempts. One of the participants, an artist I knew slightly, gave me valuable advice: "Tina, you just have to get in there and do the work. The funding will follow."

So I got in there and signed on to teach in six different classrooms spread out over three Berkeley schools. Somehow presuming myself to be a fledgling entrepreneur, I charged each teacher thirty-five dollars that they paid out of their own pockets!

I had some experience starting an arts education program. Two years before this, I had walked off the street into the Judah Magnes Museum, vaguely intending to look for a job. I had no background to support this idea. I'd been working as a part-time instructor at various colleges in the Bay Area. My claim to this teaching was founded upon a PhD in Comparative Literature. I guess I thought a Jewish museum might somehow want to hire a Hebrew scholar.

The art curator, whom I encountered first, quickly disabused me of this fantasy. She flatly told me, "We have no money." On my way out of the building, an elderly man descending the stairs asked me what I was doing there. "Looking for a job." "Come up and talk to me," he said. I had accidentally bumped into the director of the museum. He invited me to tell him about myself. I spent the next hour or so recounting stories about teaching art to kids in Cambridge, Massachusetts, Toronto, and Israel. My brother, a physicist and a doctor, had loved to hear me talk about the forty kids I drew one by one in an Open Classroom school in Cambridge, the autistic child who made an electrical outlet out of clay, keys, nails and cardboard in Boston, the Moroccan children who laughed at me when I lectured to them about art in Hebrew with a Canadian accent in back villages in Israel... Seymour liked the stories, too.

He made the following offer. If I persuaded enough teachers to bring their students to the museum, he'd look for a donor to pay me to start what he called "the first Children's Art Program." Seymour was a gambler; but he hedged his bets. I was only going to be paid for the summer. If that succeeded, he'd see about the fall. I agreed to take on the challenge.

I spent the next several weeks calling teachers. I studied the exhibits at the Magnes, looking for artistic, cultural, or historical points of interest, even when there were very few. Kathleen, an artist I knew slightly, volunteered to help me teach art. One hundred and seventy-five children from eight different summer camps, synagogues and churches signed up for the workshops between August 2 and August 25. We held classes outside in the lush museum garden on two picnic tables. I became reliant on Kathleen, who sometimes showed up attired in a dress and heels, for her excellent memory for what the children said as they made puppets or did collages or wrote illustrated comics. Kathleen, the kids, and I were in heaven.

I loved the work, however precarious the situation was. Seymour agreed to finance the fall semester. However, it was his philosophy that I should be able to do more as I got more experienced and therefore be paid less. When I presented him with an invoice that challenged this view, he wasn't pleased and later refused to find a donor for the spring. I went ahead with the work anyway and paid myself from the scanty revenues from the groups of kids that showed up at the museum.

In the winter and the spring, my workshops took place inside the building upstairs where the staff met for lunch and regular meetings. Often there was a conflict for space and, while they made room for my classes willingly after the work I did with Harold Paris in the fall (which they liked), their tolerance for my occupation of their room waned with the size of my paycheck.

When an educator position arose, probably because of the work I'd done, I applied. I wasn't selected and was brokenhearted. My youngest sister intervened at that point and told me in the way only she could do, "Tina, it's time you started something on your own."

walking lonely,
The un→ AmeRican
Dream, my freedom
is my sou|

Alex Chretien '99'

2
Children have what it takes

So I had messages from more than one source to get this work moving. And I moved. Using the model I'd worked out at the Judah Magnes Museum, I took advantage of the fact that back then schools had funding for buses to travel to museums all over the Bay Area. First I journeyed to six different museums researching various cultures — Mexican, Chinese, African, East Indian, Native American, and European — with the almost semi-conscious conviction at this point that exhibits should not merely be novelties to elementary public school children, but places of serious learning.

My sequence of five classes started with a presentation of the cultural and artistic background of each exhibit. I initiated this cultural transmission by reading illustrated stories I wrote for my goddaughter. Each story featured Carina as the protagonist engaged in some kind of exploit in relation to the culture of Muertes des Dies, Mbuti Africa, European painting, Imperial China, India, etc.

I asked my students to write and illustrate their favorite part of each story, and one group of second grade Asian students at Bella Vista School in Oakland, offered to send their illustrated stories to her.

In one story, Carina had a dream which took her to Mumbai, India. In this particular village, the women painted their mud huts, and every year, there was a festival when the people of the village threw paint at each other. Carina, too, joined in this play:

The children in my Malcolm X class took off from the exhibit of Mithila painters they saw at the Berkeley Art Museum to create marvelous paintings.

They wrote the content of their pictures around the edges of their paintings; then cut out sponges in the shape of fish, flowers, etc., and used them to print these figures in different colors throughout the remaining white spaces.

Each story was also a collaboration between me, as the writer of the story, and my friend, Bill Smock, who devoted an immense amount of time to illustrating the stories. His illustrations were culled from National Geographic magazines, the internet, and lengthy drawing sessions at museums. He even made his wife sit for him when he needed a model for a princess who appeared at the end of one of the stories.

The reading of each story was followed by a slide show of some of the art on view at the exhibit. I used a slide projector that half the time refused to "take" the slides because they were too thick. I procured many of them from the public library if the museum we visited did not offer slides. The trip to the museum was a big deal for me, the teachers, and most of all for the students. Before we even set foot in the museums, I told them they were going to an adult place, they couldn't run, they couldn't even talk. On one trip to the Asian Art Museum, an outside observer wrote a letter to the principal at Malcolm X School in Berkeley, praising the behavior of my students.

What I discovered was that it didn't take much to get these students, who often wouldn't listen to their teachers cajoling them to be quiet in their classrooms, to remain quiet and self-possessed within the walls of a museum. They became silent as soon as they entered the door. They were in awe of the buildings, the art, and me as I went to great lengths to explain what they saw, initiating my remarks with a series of Socratic questions, sometimes based on what they'd learned in the two prior classes when I prepared them for this visit. I also asked them to really look at the art and think for themselves, and they responded as no one anticipated they would. This responsiveness was my first clue to what low-income, minority kids could do when I put them in a situation that asked a lot of them.

For the final two one-and-a-half hour sessions in the classroom, I thought up visual art projects combined with writing exercises. I recall many classes, but one of the first classes really surprised me. My students made beautiful black and white paintings inspired by their tour of an Imperial Chinese exhibit. Then they wrote Chinese calligraphic poems on the side, based on a calligraphy lesson I gave them. I'd taught them to write the words for "sun," "mountain," "trees," etc. They translated their poems into English and placed the English words underneath the calligraphs. The second session they made paintings with colored tempera paint and again wrote calligraphic poems on the side; but this time they didn't write the English translations underneath, and when they stood up to show their work, they translated their poems from memory.

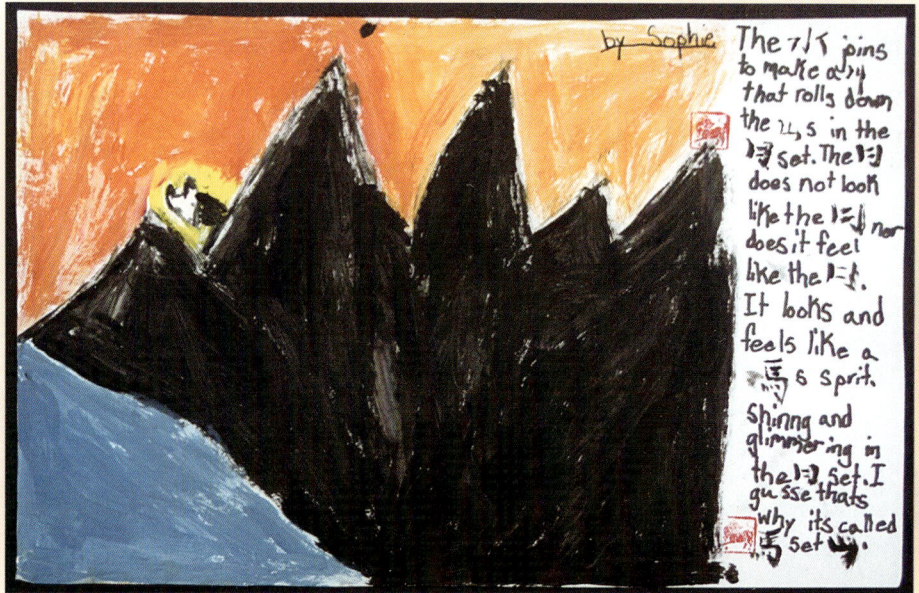

by Sophie

The 水 joins to make a ocean that rolls down the 山,s in the 月 set. The 月 does not look like the 月 nor does it feel like the 日. It looks and feels like a 馬's sprit. Shining and glimmering in the 月 set. I gusse thats why its called 馬 set.

The 月 shines so bright. On the 山s, in the dark. 水 sparkles in this pretty sight. 馬 is starting to come. But still the 馬s do not go to sleep, but in the 水 the 魚s are sleeping tight in there beds. Good night sleep tight!

Denise

It would be hard to forget that these children, and all the rest of the kids VALA artists taught, were low income, at-risk, under served — all the buzz words used to identify them and differentiate them from the white, middle-class population of children. And yet, to jump ahead several years, I've become more and more convinced that they are as capable as their more privileged peers of feats of creative and personal expression. These discoveries, piece by piece, child by child, class by class, from preschool through middle school have fueled my imagination, given me extraordinary satisfaction, and motivated me to uncover just how to best make these kids' possibilities emerge and become evident to them.

This book is a chronicle of my discoveries as well as my concern at the ways the school system, and even art educators with the best intentions, inhibit children's natural gifts and sell these children short. I long for the potential of children and youth, no matter where they come from or what language they speak, to be recognized and honored. Children have what it takes – we often don't. That's the sad truth that must be seen to give these kids back their birthright.

As an arts educator, even as a teacher, one can ask oneself, "What can I possibly do for six classes of children, even for twenty or thirty classes, when so many more are suffering from poverty, loss of their real parents, unsafe neighborhoods, and over stressed teachers struggling to teach boring, often irrelevant, standardized curricula and test them relentlessly so they won't fail the tests; because if they do, the teachers may lose their jobs?" Certainly teachers with these pressures think twice before they let an artist into their classrooms, even for six weeks, one hour a week. And yet I worked precisely with those teachers, one by one, that first year. Some helped me; some taught me a lot; some were grudging, even critical. But all of them were thrilled when they took their students to see the exhibit of the artwork of all six classrooms at the Berkeley Store Gallery where the entire huge space had been ceded to KMAWP.

When my father came to town and looked carefully through the entire exhibit, he didn't say one word until he walked out the door and muttered, "a creative explosion." I brought a number of funders to see it and I started to receive grants from the Walter & Elise Haas Fund, the East Bay Community Foundation, and others, who would support VALA for years. Nobody questioned the excellence of the show; some marveled at it. I learned, once and for all, that children seeing their own work in an exhibit space, sometimes with their parents, was the final necessary ingredient – they not only liked it, they were proud of their work.

Above is an example of the children's collages. I cut up triangles, circles and squares from magazines, and gave one shape to each child and asked them to paste them on construction paper and connect them with paint. I was trying to help them to make abstract paintings after a visit to the permanent collection at San Francisco Museum of Modern Art.

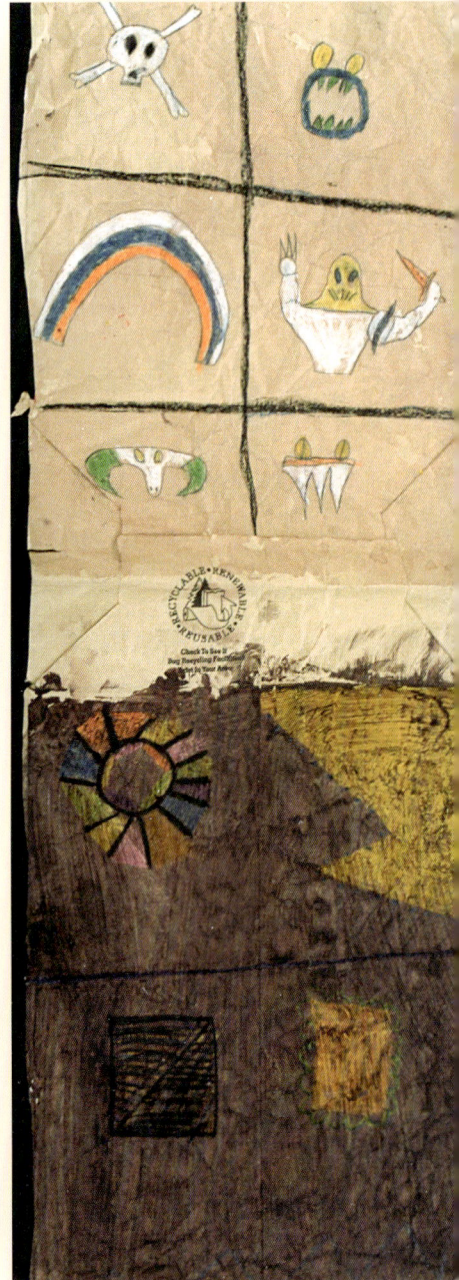

The artwork to the right stemmed from a trip to an African exhibit of Mbuti art by a kindergarten class at Oxford School. They used crayon to make the signs of the Mbuti language on brown paper bags, cut open and spread out. Then they used sponges to spread colored washes over the marks.

3
I think the bird is saying things to me that I don't even know

One of the first things I learned about the children I taught was that, after grade three, they universally hated their artwork. Grade three marked a turning point in the freedom with which they created and the way they judged their own work. In a school in Oakland Chinatown, where we taught for four years and received unprecedented financial support, the classroom teachers uncharacteristically aligned themselves with VALA artists by translating what we had to say into Mandarin and Cantonese for children who were just "off the boat" from China six months prior to entering an American elementary school.

One year I taught two third grade classrooms at this school. As usual, I went around the circle of children sitting on the floor with their artwork displayed face-up in front of them. I asked them how they liked their work and universally, to my surprise, they went around the circle saying they liked it a lot. Not quite trusting my ears, I asked them to go around the circle again and tell me how they felt. Child after child now told me, just as convincingly, "I hate my painting." There was a cultural lesson there I did not quite get, but it led me to expect a uniform judgment from these children, even if it changed each time I went around. In any case, children's evaluations of their own work were predictably negative. I only met one child, during my entire career as an art teacher, who seemed so well-adjusted that he felt happy with just about every piece of art he created.

Having said this about the tendency of children to become overly critical about their creative work by the age of nine, I had an experience with a grade four class at Coronado School in Richmond, in the Iron Triangle, which completely contradicted this generalization. I had been teaching poetry to this class for six weeks in the fall semester. I was walking my dog at dawn most days, and the days I taught the class in Richmond, I'd often make up poems in my head about what I saw and felt in the early morning light and write them down, make copies, and bring them to my class to teach them. I'm embarrassed to say this because my poems from this time were almost universally bad. But my students adopted my first lines and made poems of their own which were sometimes outstanding. One week a young African-American girl handed me a poem that was so good that I went home and typed it up and taught it the next week to this class. Here is her poem:

> I am alone in this place
> for I have left the birds' words
> and the voice of the wind sings
> to me with the rhythm of the trees
> as the music of my life
> for the one I love is beyond
> me and I am solitary and with emotion
> and confusion for I am lost
> in my thoughts. And I speak not
> for I dare to stop the wind.
>
> by Ivori H.

Ivori was a withdrawn child who usually covered her poems with her hand when I passed by to see if any children wanted help. She seldom commented in class or raised her hand to answer questions.

It is apparent how the themes of my poetry entered these children's language and became the vehicle for them to express their loneliness and isolation. Roshod informed me he was a songwriter, so I insisted he write poems, and, when I showed the following poem to his teacher, Ms. Dennis, she told me he was a foster child:

> *I am alone*
> *at this beach. I feel*
> *like I have no one*
> *to talk to.*
> *I think the bird*
> *is saying things*
> *to me that I don't*
> *even know. I feel*
> *so blue that I feel*
> *like I can cry.*
> *and that's why*
> *I will not speak*
> *to the wind.*

When I returned to the classroom in the spring semester, I waited for them in the classroom until recess ended. Then I watched all of them file in, with their heads down, in single file. When Ivori came opposite to me, she raised her head and greeted me joyfully. I felt pleased, for it seemed that I'd reached at least one child.

I decided to vary the diet of what I taught by teaching them to draw portraits. I told them to experiment with drawing what they saw — not to try to draw realistically but to vary the shape of the head, the placement of the eyes and the mouth and the ears. I suggested they draw triangles or squares for the head and put the eyes at the top of the forehead or where the mouth usually went. To my surprise, they adopted my suggestions and, though I said they could draw for as little as five minutes if they felt like it, and then start a new drawing, all of them drew for the full period of fifty minutes. I told them not to talk – a tall order for ten year olds' who had the embarrassing task of drawing their friends – for I wanted them to notice how they felt about doing these drawings and then write it down at the end.

The drawings were interesting and surprising – no conventional formulaic ways of drawing faces and features. But what was really a shock was how many children told me that they felt like "real artists" as they did their drawings; many said they felt "fantastic." So what conclusion can I draw from these children's comments? Was the instruction to focus on how they felt as they made the drawing so different from an assessment of the value of the drawings? Had I discovered a key to eliciting overwhelmingly positive responses from children over nine years of age? Was the connection I'd established with the children through teaching writing an essential predecessor to their enjoyment of making art? I was determined to take note of this class that was such an exception and discover ways of teaching poetry and the arts that would bring other children back to the sense of pleasure and satisfaction in their own creative efforts that was practically universally evident in this drawing class.

In my

vessel,

i KEEP. . . . .

the clear air of the EARTH

AND THE bacteria in pieces of dirt

i keep. . . . .
the howl in a wolf and the
SQUEAK in a mouse

4
Learning in all the arts is interconnected

Besides Sean Nash, a Native American painter who regularly held auctions of his work and gave the proceeds to VALA, Amy Trachtenberg was the primary VALA artist who was both a teacher and an activist. One of the first examples of Amy's activism included hooking me up with the head of PIXAR University (the education annex to PIXAR) after she had been hired to do an installation for PIXAR Animation Studios, one of the largest and best 3-D animation studios in the country. PIXAR ended up sending two artists for free into a fifth grade class at Cragmont School in Berkeley to teach students animation. I'll never forget what that classroom was like with these two PIXAR artists making storyboards of the students' ideas and drawings. The excitement was so high that at times it verged on outright pandemonium. From the children's drawings, the artists created professional drawings back at the studios that they displayed the following week in the classroom. At the end of five sessions, the kids were transported by a bus, paid for by PIXAR, to the animation studios to see the animation film the artists had created from the students' work.

Amy's work in the community also included an installation in the atrium at Children's Hospital in Oakland. She made sure that a series of walls were reserved to hang children's art, and we were invited to hang the first exhibit of children's art in this space.

It has been my experience that certain artists elicit the finest art from their students. Amy was one of these. She taught them serious drawing and painting, emphasizing direct observation of still lifes and figures, whether they were looking at a vessel or drawing their own hands. Here are some examples of the art work done by her fourth grade students at Lincoln School in Oakland:

IN My Philip vesssell

I keep dinosaur, fire ant, ostrich, alligator, cloud, pillow, iron, panda

She also took several classes to museum exhibits of different cultures and worked out sophisticated ideas presenting a range of different conceptions of art to second, third, and fourth grade children.

The first series of classes Amy taught was based on a Ben Shahn exhibit at the Judah Magnes Museum. She emphasized the political nature of Shahn's depression-era posters and taught her students to create paintings of homeless people in black tempera paint, based on photographs and paintings she brought in of people in various postures, standing, reclining, sitting. She made several Xerox copies of each child's painting that they then painted in color. I led the kids in a session of talking about homelessness and writing paragraphs about homeless people. Then Amy, the classroom teacher, and I went around helping the kids pick out the best line from their paragraph to write on strips of paper and then paste across their posters. It was no surprise that the results of this class were chosen for the Youth Art Exhibit at the Berkeley Art Center that year. Here are a couple of the posters:

In the fall semester of 1999, Amy took two second grade classes at Malcolm X in Berkeley to visit the exhibit, "The Art of the Sikh Kingdom" at the Asian Art Museum in San Francisco. To prepare her students for the trip to the museum, she showed them slides of her own work in mixed media and collage as well as slides of temple sculpture, textiles, arms, and painting. She talked about the way that a culture's stories and history can be shown and learned through art. Her preparation for the visit and tour of the exhibit was elaborate.

In the third session, she brought in five distinct objects for the students to sketch using charcoal. Amy's description gives some idea of how she managed to get children to make such great drawings: "They were all vessels and had an unusual form or detail that engaged all of the students. Repeatedly they drew the objects; some in a more sustained and detailed manner and others with fluid rapidity composing several objects together on the page. Charcoal was the medium. It is bold and forgiving and most every child had never encountered this basic medium before. I stressed repeatedly that this was an exercise in looking, not about making great drawings. I see sketching as a form of note-taking and training the eye and hand to record what they see. They were prolific, allowed to move around to different tables to draw different objects. Their drawings are astonishing."

It's apparent that the unexpected quality and range of Amy's students is a direct consequence of the careful thought and attention she gave to her lessons as well as her mode of carrying out what she does. In the best VALA tradition, Amy's students went beyond all her expectations; and yet this could not have happened if Amy had not designed a series of classes which expected far more of her students than most artists ever anticipate from young children.

Amy continues, "Session four was begun with the reading of a Sikh poem. All of the children read with me and some of them made motions acting out the scale or objects evoked in the poem. Then I read to them with their eyes closed. Each child then generated a few poem lines of their own related to something or someone they were devoted to as well as thinking about the sky. A mandala project was introduced. I showed two examples of collages made with printed Chinese paper and cut cloth glued around and inside of a series of circles like a target. I had found these blue line targets printed and thought they would be interesting as a base. We talked about found materials and old paper and patterns. They recopied some of their words into the mandala as an additional pattern element.

In session five they used very large recycled manila envelopes as the base for their watercolor paintings and applied fabric collages. The paintings were supposedly based on their writing, though some of the children responded with different imagery once they got involved with the paint. They finished these by adding and gluing pieces of silky and velvet fabrics to highlight their painting. I was most impressed with the uniqueness of each individual student's work. There was no copying and a wide range of expression resulted."

In a second grade class at Bella Vista in Oakland, Amy demonstrated just how beautiful children's work with patterns could be:

Amy went on to create many more projects for children and finally she collaborated with poet, Pat Reed. Pat is both a fine poet and a first-rate teacher and she could figure out steps in teaching everyone from elementary school children to adult teachers to write poems like Gertrude Stein did in **Tender Buttons**. They learned from each other, and children wrote poems and did art as never before. One series of classes designed and taught by Amy and Pat together has the following title:

Painting and Poetry from Life
Water, Sky, Moods, and Light

For this series of classes, Amy first introduced herself and presented slides of paintings with the emphasis on unusual light and color in the landscape. She discussed with the class some of the ways painters work with light and color. Then Pat asked the class to see if they could tell time of day, season, climate, and mood in each painting, and what clues told them this. They then chose a painting to write from and composed a group poem that Pat wrote on the board. Pat and Amy took turns teaching their classes, overlapping and building on each other's presentations. They became so attached to working together that one would agree to teach a class or lead a workshop only if the other were there too. So they were finding themselves as teachers of young children in each other's company.

This example of team teaching by an artist and a poet, that Amy and Pat perfected, further substantiates the underlying premise behind VALA that learning in all the arts is interconnected and poetry complements every other form of creativity.

5
The sky is a path
you can't find it

I had a plan for transforming all VALA artists into teachers of poetry by reading and discussing poems with them in my living room. I have had some successes teaching performing artists to use writing — poetry — as a spur to creativity. This plan had worked with Veronica Williams, an African-American dancer. She had taught the Chilean poet, Gabriel Mistral, and the African-American songwriter, Gil Scott Heron, to students at a middle school in Oakland.

She had first requested a poet who wrote in Spanish for her class composed of largely Spanish-speaking Latino sixth graders. We went over Mistral's poem in detail. Veronica was a serious teacher and an even more serious student. She was receptive to my analysis of "Rain," and curious about how she could interweave the elements of dance with her teaching of the poem. The impromptu lesson was demanding for both of us.

Veronica taught dance from the interior lives of her students outwards to their physical bodies. She often used extended visualizations. As a way of introducing them to Mistral's poem about the rain, she asked her students to imagine they were in a flood. One student wrote about this experience as follows: "I was looking out my window just looking at the rain. Wanting it to stop. Half a day passes and it's still raining. It looks like it's about to flood the street. I panicked and just stayed in the house and just looked at the water flooding the street. All you see is water now, nothing else than water. Water starts coming in the house. You panic and try to hide. Then the water picks up your house and now your house is floating. It starts floating to a magical place with bright colors and beautiful animals. Then you start to float the other way. Now you're back where you were, where you were looking at the rain." Some dance choreography, and then he wrote the following poem:

This land, great and big
like an animal whose
Finding its way.

Will you sleep, with
the suffering of the
water sounds
like the roars of
the lion.

Soft as bamboo in the wind
and fierce like in battle.

This shadow in the deep mother
earth can't be found but
they can hear a loud sound.

The sky is a path
you can't find it
but travels on and on.

Other students responded by writing some exceptional poems. I was optimistic that more VALA artists who weren't writers could do what Veronica had been able to do.

But the success was not automatic. Early in the fall of 2007, I met with Leon Kassapides, a Greek shadow play puppeteer. Leon is one of the members of the San Francisco shadow theater company, ShadowLight Productions. He performs all over the US and Europe.

I presented a poem to Leon from a chapbook by Pat Reed set in the California wilderness of rivers, sunrises, snakes, frogs, and deer. It was the task of each artist to work with themes from the district literacy curriculum. Leon's unit was "City Wildlife." We stretched our connections to these themes, for Pat's poem was situated far from any city landscape.

Leon received my comments about the poem enthusiastically. He proposed making it the basis for his students' performances. I thought he meant that they would compose their scripts from the language of the poem, and the elements of the poem — animals, river, trees — would be the "characters" populating the shadow theater.

I made a point of showing up for Leon's final class. He'd taught a series of six classes over the span of one week. I was looking forward to witnessing the results of this intensive work. The principal of the school was there along with another grade three teacher and all his students. We formed a substantial audience.

Leon read Pat's poem at the beginning. His students performed the pieces they'd written in small groups behind a large piece of white paper that Leon slung from the rafters. They had mastered the theatrical part of the shadow puppetry quite well. Their titles were interesting, though tangentially inspired by the poem. But the words of the scripts were abysmally boring.

The following conversation was a typical example:

> *Hi. How are you?*
> *I'm fine. How are you?*
> *What are you doing?*
> *I'm watching TV. What are you doing?*

Leon had set up the class so that the audience could ask questions and comment after each performance. The children regarded me quizzically when I burst out with, "You can write much better! I know you can." I'm familiar with the widened eyes of surprised children, but I had to wonder if they knew what I was driving at.

Still, I followed my hunch. That day I went up to Leon and told him I'd come to one of his next series of classes to teach writing. He didn't catch my drift that moment, but the next time I told him, he reacted fiercely against my proposal: "I've been teaching for 18 years, and I don't want you to teach any of my classes." I realized I had to proceed more carefully, and, undaunted, I wrote him a formal letter, offering my teaching demonstration as a "gift, not something I want to impose on you." I explained that I had a doctorate in literature, was a poet (published), and had been working with kids in the arts for 34 years. He capitulated. We made plans for me to show up for one class.

I don't know where I got my audacity. I now had to prove myself to these kids and an internationally known artist, and I didn't want to lose face with either. I had my belief that the kids could do much better and, if I succeeded with them, Leon might turn out to be a VALA artist who could teach shadow theater and writing. It now seemed like showing up and doing it would be the only way to transmit this skill to him. I'd tried teaching him a poem in my living room. It had failed.

On that morning I was faced with the children, Leon, and a formidable classroom teacher. Ms. Jeanie Harris was an older African-American teacher who made her students stand up to speak and answer questions with complete sentences. My first step was to politely but firmly negotiate with Ms. Harris. "My" students should not have to stand up or speak in complete sentences. It seemed to me that kids answered questions quickly, in a rush. I didn't want to inhibit them. I felt learning should have a spontaneity to it. After some resistance, she gave in on both counts.

I read the Grimms fairy-tale, "Bremen Town Musicians," to the children while they followed along with their own copies. As I began to question them, these well-trained students both stood up and, for the most part, answered in complete sentences. What surprised even me was the sophistication of their language and their thinking. This old-school teacher had taught them to stand, to speak, and to think.

In the story, four different animals, mistreated by their masters, decided to go together to Bremen to become musicians. I asked them to invent conversations between one of the animals and its master that antedated the story.

Typical of my experience of teaching creative writing to kids, there was a tense period between the time I gave them their writing task and when they actually "got" it and began to write. No matter how many times I teach kids, this lag time always feels difficult to me. I think, "nothing is going to happen." They aren't going to grasp even the initial steps of what they are asked to do. They seem completely baffled.

I've come to believe that this interval of doubt is an essential part of my teaching. I try to do something the children don't usually do so something new will take place. But I'm faced with the possibility that my excessive effort will fall flat, and this moment of my feeling like a failure is actually a precondition for their writing to take off.

As far as I can tell, this tension is the key to what I hope VALA artists will be able to do. Success as a teacher is based on the attempt, over and over again, to go beyond where the kids and their teachers imagine they can go.

This time lapse is actually somewhat of a mystery to me. What transpires in these children's minds between the moment they feel absolutely lost and in the dark about what I ask them to write and the moment they begin to write? When the children seem baffled, classroom teachers often step in and explain my assignment in simpler terms. The best teachers seem equipped to know what their students can and can't understand. I feel, at those times, like a fool, shown up by a teacher who knows better than I just what their students can understand. However, while the teacher appears to help get them started, I'm not sure this assistance is the main force behind the movement that always comes sooner or later.

Sometimes a child I try to help tells me "I'm thinking." Then I feel like a different kind of fool. Why didn't I think of this? Of course they need time to think. Why did I imagine their "stalling" meant they weren't doing anything?

I've also come to realize that the time I spend with each individual child — coaxing, explaining, showing how — is far more important than any carefully planned lesson in front of the whole class at the beginning. So the point at which I meet each child is critical to launching a poem, a dialogue, a title, a story. For each child requires his/her own unique piece of instruction, and each piece of writing is best responded to differently from every other piece, for no child's writing is like any other's. Each child has his own quintessential identity. They respond to this differentiation.

That day in Ms. Harris' classroom, the kids did start to write their conversations between the animals and their masters. The dialogues then became the scripts for the shadow theater they did that semester. All three adults became exuberant as we watched several children in turn get up to read their writing. My work with them softened Ms. Harris' attitude toward me and impressed Leon.

The effort was intense and demanding. Yet if even the least verbal of Ms. Harris' kids could write, I persuaded myself that I could pass my teaching before the eyes of other dubious VALA artists and Richmond teachers.

6
It was hard for me
not to start dancing

Leon Kassapides completed his teaching of shadow theater to Ms. Jeanie Harris' class with a renewed sense of enthusiasm. His next series of six classes took place in Mr. Larouchette's third grade class. It was his students who had formed the audience for Ms. Harris' performers. But even Leon was not prepared for just how ready these students were. He narrates as follows: "To be honest I was nervous about reading them the poem 'Sirens & Flashing Lights Stop' from the Allen Ginsberg collection of *Poems for the Nation:*

> *traffic where the strikers tried*
> *to stop trucks plowing thru*
> *their human wall*
> *& cops waded into*
> *the jobless lines*
> *collaring shouting men & women,*
> *tossing them into the wagons*
> *& slamming the doors:*
> *high noon*
> *in the shadowless summer,*
> *unseen eyes*
> *peering thru the mirrored windows*
> *where others, jobless*
> *for years of scrambling*
> *part-timers & sweepers*
> *to pay the rising*
> *rent and fill the hungry mouths*
> *succumb to the scab siren's song of money.*

He writes, "It was hard for me not to start dancing or moving around and jumping with this powerful, very visual poem." Leon had handed me Ginsberg's collection of poems some weeks before and told me that he'd be willing to teach any of them to his next class of children. I selected the one quoted above. Leon describes what happened after he read the poem:

"I asked them if they understood what the poet was talking about and, to my surprise, they did. Not only did they understand, but they also used words such as "strike", "union", "boycott". I was very impressed, and Mr. L told me that they studied Cesar Chavez and his organizing of the grape farmhand strikes for a month earlier in the school year." Leon explained the next steps of the process. He'd divided them into groups and then each group would design and create shadow puppets and scenery and write their own stories, and on the sixth day of the residency, they'd perform live in front of an audience, using the overhead projector and everyday classroom materials.

On the second day, Leon decided to invite the kids to make up some oral free-form stories and poems about what happened to the people in the poem before and after the visual scene that it describes. He was clearly influenced by the idea of imagining what happened before the "Bremen Town Musicians" story. Since he has the context of shadow theater to work with, he can go beyond just asking the kids to write a story. They place their imaginations into the "pot" of designing characters and scenery and then dramatize their writing. He continues: "Everybody was very imaginative about creating directions for where the struggle for life improvement can go. Fatima's group made up a story of all animal characters with many healthy planet and recycling concepts. Jesus' play was about how people shouldn't be cruel to animals even when they farm them for meat. Carolina and her colleagues talked about a family that has to move around in different towns because the boss doesn't treat them fairly and they can't make enough money to pay the rent. Eventually they organize many families and they like their working environment. Ayallie and her friends talked about a shoe factory where the workers strike and form a union to get what they want." It was evident to Leon that the kids' personal issues were surfacing in their stories.

The rest of the second day he explained to them that the puppets needed to be designed in profile and that they had to pay special attention to the noses of their characters because in puppetry that feature conveys information about the intensity and personality of the specific character. Then he demonstrated movement and entrances and exits, and the kids took turns improvising short scenes with puppets that he'd brought with him to the class.

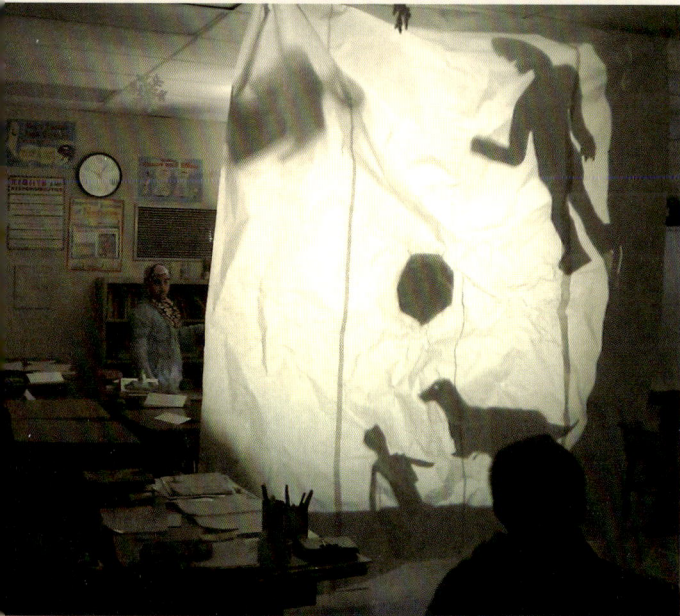

So Leon teaches these children techniques for projecting their cut out puppets and scenery on the screen by manipulating them in front of a light source. He describes some of the ways he also teaches them to dramatize their poems:

"Basically I taught them that although it's fun to have a scene going on and on with two or more characters arguing, at the end it's better when the characters don't block each other while disagreeing. This way the story can continue and we care about our audience, entertaining them and teaching them."

The final section of Leon's account reveals how many things the kids learned from this experience: "I reminded everyone what they should pay attention to: be louder, don't bump the scenery with the puppets, the puppet that talks moves, the puppet that listens stays still, entrances and exits are important. The audience arrived and then Diego stood in front of the screen and read the poem in the style of poetry slams where the poet performs the poem. He projected his voice and used many emotional gestures... After this dynamic introduction, the performance of 'The Unhappy Shoemaker' with Fatima's group started. The scenery was incredible; the contour lines of the factory and the workers' tools were economical, balanced, and powerful. Diego's reading of the poem influenced the spirit of the young activist actors."

For the story about Cesar Chavez and the grape farmers, "Carolina used different sizes of shadow puppets to show depth and three-dimensionality on a flat screen. I could see that everyone's language skills had improved and, although I gave them the option of performing in Spanish (their first language), everybody performed in English." Leon continues, "Jesus' group demonstrated a virtuosity of improvisation and ability to listen to the audience's reaction. The performers improved their script on the spot by feeling the audience's energy. At one point when the farmer invited in the cow, but instead the pig entered, and then he said, 'you are the pig not the cow,' the audience started laughing. The actors held for laughs, which is a theater rule that they obeyed by instinct during their actual performance." Most importantly, Leon concludes that the children effectively conveyed the meaning of the piece — that you can farm in a more respectful way and even animals can organize a union and strike and boycott hay feeding by refusing to work in the fields.

Leon concludes his account of this teaching experience with the following words:

"My shadow theater class keeps evolving. I feel that my students teach me different approaches and techniques in education. What I did very differently in the productions of these shadow plays is that when a scene would need help and improvement I would actually move from my audience member's seat, then go backstage and give them suggestions while they performed. Without missing a beat these students would take my whispering suggestions of dramaturgy and turn it into magical shadows."

It is interesting to me that Leon confided in a footnote in his previous evaluation that he had been born in 1966, and for Kindergarten and Grade One, he went to public schools in downtown Thessaloniki, Greece. The boys had to shave their heads and the teachers included a lot of hitting in their discipline practices. His mother didn't want his head to be shaved and so he was moved to a private school. But even in this school "there was a serious amount of hitting" and the kids were made to "memorize every subject as it was written in the books as if we were robots." From the little chance I had to get to know Leon, one of the things that struck me about him was that he could be very playful and had the imagination of a child. In other words, being with him felt safe, as though I was with someone who understood what it was to be like a child. His grasp of shadow theater is, of course, sophisticated. No wonder his students blossomed and came to perform strong shadow puppetry, and no wonder he could learn so well from my one example. He knew what it was to learn like a child and to teach like a master.

7
Nothing around me except me

In April of 2008, I met Janet Stevens, a new artist who was teaching capoeira martial art to fourth graders, in the office of Cesar Chavez School in Richmond. Janet generally appears self-contained and, at times, perhaps a little withdrawn, except when she came to my house to discuss her class. Her plan for these classes, which she submitted to me well in advance of her starting date, was superb. She was also one of the new VALA artists who put up no resistance to my demonstrating the teaching of poetry to her students. I was excited by this opportunity to "remake" a willing artist by adding poetry to her arsenal of skills. That day Janet greeted my enthusiastic gratitude for her willingness to accept me into her class with the caveat, "but I am not a teacher of poetry."

I paused for a second to absorb her modest qualification and then introduced myself to Persida, the classroom teacher. She informed me that she got her students to memorize and recite poems once a month. I praised her, wondering what poems she taught, and offered to send her poems to teach. Accidentally I happened to look up at a bookshelf and saw the title, *Emily Dickinson for Children*.

Janet's plan had been able to include my poetry class. She used the district's literacy theme of "Survival" as a point of departure from which to bring her students to a new sense of playfulness and fearlessness through capoeira moves. She told me she had tried to relate to her students her own feeling of freedom and joy when she did capoeira. The previous class was called "capoeira as an expression of my uniqueness." She had decided that my class would come under the heading of "poetry as an expression of my uniqueness."

I chose a poem from Pat Reed's collection **Tangle Blue,** which I felt came closer to my sense of myself now than many of my own poems. Here is the poem:

> *Waking on my*
> *dark heart*
> *in the cloud strewn*
> *dawn*
>
> *I struggle to stand*
> *in the green*
> *stillness*
>
> *the frogs*
> *start their jerky*
> *amble back down*
> *to the water*
>
> *and the oneness*
> *of the sun*
>
> *accepts my one,*
>
> *puts light*
> *on the skin*
> *of the water*

I started with an explanation of internal rhyme and alliteration and pointed out how they tied together the different parts of the poem. I asked the meaning of the image "dark heart" and as usual, they came up with many answers, ranging from the color of the ground to a sad mood. I always ask open-ended questions and accept many different interpretations, frequently learning new possibilities that I hadn't thought of. I explained that the poet links the "dark" earth with the brightness of the "stars" through the metaphor of "garden of stars."

I asked them, "How can stillness be green? What does she see around her? Do you know what it's like to wake up at dawn when everything is still?"

I had chosen the poem as an expression of who I was because of the lines "and the oneness/of the sun/accepts my one." I struggled with these students for a while to get them to comprehend this mystical union between the poet/perceiver and the natural world. I asked the question, "Did you ever look at something or someone so hard that you lost a sense of being yourself and became what you looked at?" Their responses ranged far and wide until one child, Michelle, narrated her experience of sitting in front of a campfire and looking at the fire at night until everything disappeared but the fire. Michelle says it far better than I can:

Waking on my dark heart when
the clouds were gray.
When I see a campfire everything goes away.
All I see is darkness all around me
Nothing else is there except one light
with wood burning
All I see is light and everything disappears.
Nothing around me except me.

I was always worried about bringing poems like this one about camping in the wilderness to inner-city children. But I soon discovered that Persida had taken them on a camping trip two weeks before. My admiration for Persida soared! Nareap picked up the essence of this experience of looking as a kind of self-dissolution:

Waking on my
goat boat
On the sunny
evening

next to the goats
princess peanut butter
cookies and coffee

I tried to get out of the
boat but I could not

When I looked I felt like I was not
my self and
then it was night.

I had talked about the experience of looking at a tree or a flower in the light of a sunrise when it feels as though you see the world for the first time; or, what happens when you look at someone with love and see how they are beautiful, even when they might first strike you as ugly.

Then another inimitable lyric came through Carlos' assemblage of words:

Sleeping on my
sleeping bag
rolled and
lay down

dark and foggy
I woke up
in a forest standing.

The trees make a figure
on the dark forest

accepts my one

The sun rises
The wind wakes
me up.

As frequently happens, Andrea adopts several words and motifs from Reed's poem to create her own personal poem, "Bright Light".

BRIGHT LIGHT

Sitting on my
cold bed
in the sunny
morning
I fear to stand
on the hard, cold floor
The birds
start their own singing
I lie back down
on my bed
and the oneness
of the sun
accepts me,
bright light like a
shadow
lights upon the skin of
my
cold bed.

In "Dreaming", Jonathon shifts to a sense of finding himself disoriented as he first wakes up.

DREAMING

There I was
Thinking on my couch

Thought I was asleep
I was asleep!
I wake up thinking I was at
my dad's house

I had a hard time opening my eyes
I finally opened my eyes
something was strange
about the place I was in

The house looked like
my dad's house
The walls were green
the floor was full of carpets
a tv and a bed
I thought I was crazy!
I finally I realized
I really was at
my dad's house
I was at my real home.

Oralia takes the morning awakening to a new level. It's not the place that orients her, but her mother. I had asked the children to describe themselves in a place where they are close to something or someone, so close that they forget themselves and become something else. Some children appeared at a loss to write about a special place. So I went through a list of people and asked them if they felt close to that person. I had asked Oralia, "Do you feel close to your sister? Do you have a brother? Do you feel close to your mother?" A child might seem depressed by the first option I gave her, but after I went through a list of possibilities, she'd perk up and set to writing. This is what Oralia wrote:

I feel connected
to my mother

She stands
for me through
good or bad

Laying on my
cold old bed
wondering
what will happen
next

My mother opens my
curtains to let
the light heat on
my shivering in

At the end of each day
a kiss good night

until the next moon
comes my beautiful light

I fell in love with this class, exhilarated by their responses to my questions and their lovely poems. But I pretty much forgot about my VALA artist for whose sake I was there. Janet had written a poem too and read it aloud along with the children. This level of involvement was somewhat unusual, especially since I had only casually suggested to her that she do this. She read her own poem diffidently. It combined a close attention to visual details with a ready openness to expressing difficult feelings.

Janet carried this combination into her teaching of the poem in the following class. I gathered later that she had been successful in teaching Reed's poem to her students from the poems her students wrote which she sent to me. Here are a few examples:

Waking of the
sound of birds
I see the
warm flower

As soon as the
flower glows
I can see the
darkness ahead.

But my spirit
glows like a night
sky.

As soon I see
my world outside

I think about the
wonders inside.

Janet couldn't have told me more directly that she was able to communicate to this child the form of Reed's poem, a sensory aliveness, and a profound sense of relationship between the natural world and an interior state.

And Angel imagines her way into a new sense of her own possibilities:

I was tired of walking
until I saw the giant
with its big green leaves
and its big long brown trunk
as soon as I saw that giant
I wanted to climb into the
top It got me full of
excitement the sun shines
bright on its leaves and some
day I will succeed.

I had told the class that I taught for my VALA artist that they were all poets and when they grew up, if I were still alive, I'd hire them to teach in my organization. One of the children who stands out for me from this class and from every class I've ever taught, was a beautiful little Latino girl who spoke to me after the class was over, as I lingered in the classroom, waiting for the children to copy their poems for me. Jhamilet's first words to me were, "I'm going to be a poet when I grow up." After this pronouncement, she confided that she went everywhere with a friend she'd made up. She continued, "My mother left me with my father for ten days when I was four years old. My father is bad. He went away and left me all alone." She told me her father was now in jail.

This is Jhamilet's poem:

*When I was on my heart
my deepest heart inside my heart
it was beautiful like a
beautiful flower inside
it had light like the sun
everything got quite alone
in my deepest, beautiful
heart I was not startle
I believed on my deepest
beautiful heart I had
someone that you cannot
see it's my friend she's
always beside me even if
you cannot see her do not
be scare on your heart
believe on your beautiful
heart always.*

I had, as I said, told the class that they were already poets. I didn't expect anyone to believe me, let alone anticipate my statement the way Jhamilet did. I asked her if her mother protected her. She said she did and now she had a stepfather. She also told me that she still had her imaginary friend.

I had gone to the school to say something about who I was. I found children who understood and one child who knew so well what it felt like to lose the connection with a parent that she created one who was always beside and within her. Jhamilet discovered her imaginary friend in a fraught moment of danger when she lost her father. All these children confront frightening circumstances on a more or less regular basis. Reed's poem became the occasion for them to remember and celebrate a sense of safety, pleasure, and closeness to people and places that mattered to them. By conjuring up these memories and sense perceptions in their poems, they relived them that day in Persida's class and in Janet's subsequent class.

The chain of instruction seemed to be working. From me to the children and Janet, from Janet to her children, and then on again to more children.

8
From my students I learned much more than I can say

"I have a balloon I blow up and I tell them to imagine the balloon in their belly and to blow it up, they must fill their belly with air. They must fill their belly with air when they breathe in. Then I let the air out of the balloon to demonstrate what it is like to exhale out. They put their hands on their bellies and practice the balloon breathing. I tell them when they breathe out to pretend they are blowing out a birthday candle...."

In this way, Yofe Johnson gathers her twenty-eight preschool students into the practice of yoga at Riverside School in San Pablo. Not only are they carried by Yofe's gentle manner into learning yogic breathing and postures, but also she appeals to their imaginations to join her in moving their shoulders up and down while they breathe, holding them near their ears "like a monkey" and swinging their arms back and forth.

She talks with them about animals in the jungle and they learn to imitate some of their movements. Yofe continues her description of what they do: "I teach them how to stretch their arms above them from side to side like an elephant's trunk. They drink water from the river with this trunk and then spray the water on us all. Our next exercise is to brush the water off all of our bodies, starting at the head and working our way down to our feet, brushing and shaking it all off as we name the body parts, sensing our bodies and stimulating our proprioceptic awareness."

Clearly, this teacher is right there with these children, sensing their possibilities, and leading them into new awareness of their bodies and their minds; for in this particular class, they bring a willingness to doing yoga and an excitement about what they're learning that they bring home to their mothers. When she asks them at the beginning of the third class whether any of them did yoga at home last week, most of them agree that they did the "elephant" or the "balloon breath."

Seamlessly, Yofe takes them into a new kind of stretch and a new series of associations at the end of the third class as they "sit on the floor in the position of the butterfly, soles touching each other, we flap our knees up and down, sitting on the floor, but in our mind's eye, we are flying. We then cradle each leg, hugging it close to our chest as if it were a small baby or a doll and we rock back and forth stretching the hip sockets."

What feels special to me, as I read what Yofe writes about her classes, and yet, just right, that she is so close to these students that there is no gap between what she asks them to do, what she demonstrates, and how that develops through each class, and from one class to the next. It is as though she enters into the minds of these three and four-year-olds, and sits there on her square on the rug and becomes one of them, only with an adult eye to witness and record what's happening.

How Yofe deals with any disruption of these classes fits exactly with everything else that happens here:

"Today, a new three-year-old student has joined the class. It is Mario's first day of preschool. There is barely enough room for all twenty-eight students on the carpet. Mario sits near me with one of the aides helping him. We begin with simple stretches and breathe in and out with our arms moving up and down. We do the "elephant," the "butterfly", and sing "Rock-A-Bye Baby" to our legs. Mario follows along perfectly with great coordination and motor skills. The class is asking to do the "lion," so naturally we sit on our knees, we spread our fingers out like big paws, look up and all together breathe in, and with great enthusiasm and strength, let out a big roar with tongues pointing down and out. Mario bursts into tears as the fierceness of lions surprises him. All the students feel badly that we scared him. We collectively decide to do a tiny baby lion sound, which we do, while Mario continues to sob. Mario is taken out of the circle and comforted and quieted as we continue our yoga."

But it is not just this particular preschool class in San Pablo where Yofe does yoga practice with three- and four-year-olds, but also in a preschool class for "emotionally challenged" children in an adjacent classroom. Here Yofe was confronted by a very different picture:

"In the first class, we sat on the floor in a circle and introduced ourselves. This was their first time sitting on the floor together as well as the first time they were to say their names to a stranger. They were very cooperative, except for Jmari, who cried. As we began, Andrew, an autistic child, became very involved in the repetitive movements while Mia, who has left-side paralysis, could mimic my every move perfectly with her right side. Nathan, who uses a wheelchair, needed assistance sitting up, so I supported him and moved his body to show the others how to stretch their arms up to the sky. He loved the physical contact and was very affectionate."

With this small group of students, constant strategizing to find ways for them to do the yoga movements became necessary. So with Anthony, who had an imbalance from a rare disease that caused his arms and legs to be floppy and impaired his sense of gravity, Yofe found that moving with a partner — another student, an aide, the teacher or herself — often solved the problem for him and others unable to move on their own. Movements that stretched their spines or their arms, or moves to stimulate the left and right cerebral hemispheres, such as moving legs alternately in and out while sitting and adding the arms for the more adept, were selected. She could no longer proceed in a smooth, intuitive trajectory; she had to employ all her skills in the service of working with severely handicapped children.

They played with hopping on one foot and jumping like a frog to reestablish the up/down neural pathways and to enhance balance. Adding a "ribbit" to make it more fun, and including language like "hop, hop, hop" or clapping hands, all help in the development or phrasing for speech. Yofe discovered that "some children responded more to sound. Lucas and Anthony liked to roar like a lion and felt empowered when they were all roaring together."

Together with the classroom teacher, Linda, who was an invaluable resource in charting this new territory, Yofe tried to acknowledge and praise the students "as long as they made an effort", cheering them on "for every positive move they made." With these students "there were no mistakes." From these students, Yofe learned "much more….than I can say."

I was reminded of an experience I had teaching autistic children in Boston at the Lindemann Mental Health Center in 1974. It was the hardest teaching job I ever had. It only lasted six months, and it taught me more than any other teaching job about how to teach disadvantaged children. What those five children had in common with children in Richmond and San Pablo would be hard to pin down. But the experience of tuning in to children who defy our usual expectations of how people respond prepared me for working with children who have difficulty paying attention, who tend to wander and become unruly.

Yofe went on to teach nine-year-olds in San Pablo and Richmond. For these children, who are mostly Hispanic, there is a large English language component in watching Yofe model the movements and talk them through the various phases of the poses. Navigating her three third grade classes was a new experience for her and she had to adapt to the radically different classroom styles of the teachers as well as the temperaments of their students. As with the preschool children, here Yofe stimulates her class to fantasize about the insects and animals she compares their poses to. She asks them what butterflies like to eat as they sit on the floor with the soles of their feet together, knees gently bouncing up and down like a butterfly, and one boy says "nectar," a girl says "flowers." She questions them further: "What do their butterflies like to eat?" Jose says "cheeseburgers;" Angele says "candy." Yofe comments humorously, "others agreed with the menu."

At the close of her first third grade classroom, Yofe asks her students if yoga has helped them in other parts of their lives. Some say that they are more relaxed and don't get as upset. "I can do the lion and after I roar I feel better," says Jose. Marguerite says, "the owl makes me relax." And Rachel says she remembers to breathe when she gets afraid or uncomfortable and it helps her.

Then Yofe concludes this class in a style that accords with the peaceful and healing nature of her teaching: "We row the boat towards each other into the center of the circle. We carefully move one step at a time in almost touching and then I bring them back by stepping backwards three giant steps; we then row the boat to the center breathing out as we push our arms forward and breathing in as we bring them in towards our shoulders. As we get closer and closer we push our arms toward the sky and touch hands."

The end of this first classroom experience is then connected to the opening of Yofe's second class at Wilson elementary school in San Pablo in the teacher Elaine's classroom: "I tell them yoga is very good for their bodies and helpful in calming their minds when they are nervous or afraid… When our breath is relaxed and even, our minds and thus our emotions become calm and we are able to deal with stress more effectively."

Elaine is more involved with the class than the previous teacher and her eagerness to learn yoga has an impact on the whole class. "We begin stretching and reaching, waking up our bodies. Elaine joins the class today and says she still cannot breathe correctly. She wants to learn and the children try to teach their teacher."

I counsel VALA artists on the importance of asking the classroom teachers to join in their workshops when they first meet with them and talk about what they are planning to do. Classroom teachers can make or break a class just by how interested they are in what we do. Students take their cue from their teachers, and if they consider our work valuable and participate in the class, their students follow suit. The days are gone when we ask teachers to act primarily as managers of classroom chaos. We recognize how significant the teachers' role is in carrying on our work after we leave, and we're building into our teaching time periods when the classroom teacher takes over and, with our guidance, teaches the art form we have modeled.

In the next series of classes that Yofe taught at Grant School in Richmond, it was imperative that the teacher be engaged, as the children were quite unruly and had trouble calming down and focusing. This is what Yofe faced when she came to Billie's classroom:

> *"It is a very hot afternoon when I arrive to the classroom. The teacher, Billie, welcomes me and introduces me to her students. Because the room is so hot, she suggests we try to do yoga outside in a white circle painted on the black asphalt. I agree that maybe we could try to do some of the standing poses there and come inside for the floor exercises. Once outside, it is complete chaos. The children can't hear me so I'm talking loudly and then they are screaming and running around. A few are trying to listen to me, and then the teacher is trying to quiet them down."*

Yofe copes with the noise level and the lack of attention just as she figured out how to teach physically handicapped and autistic children. Once an artist has learned to adapt her teaching to the most difficult population, she finds that all other challenges soon become manageable. She writes, "The noise level in their classroom is very high, so it's more difficult to get their attention. Their teacher raised her hand in the silence symbol, but to no avail. She then raised her voice above their collective din and they looked at her after a moment of silence as she lectured them on listening and being respectful. We then began to do some more active movements to dissipate their excessive energy level... We fling our arms this way and wrap them around our waist front and back in a big arc. We learn about the strength we have from moving from our centers and the origin of this is based on tai chi and martial arts..."

The introduction of the sun salutation pose turned out to be a valuable way of directing these kids' energy. Once tried, Yofe got them to do it over and over again: "We practice the sun salutation which requires twelve movements breathing in as we stretch open and exhaling on each contraction… We move through them slowly to feel each pose inside our bodies and then we do them faster which is easier to flow from one to the other."

Though not experienced as a teacher of poetry, Yofe was able to elicit some nice lyric poems from the students in her three classes. It seems that her transmission of her yoga lessons, combined with exercising her students' imaginations, prepared them for playful, whimsical writing. Yofe read the Rumi poem she chose twice and discussed with them the use of metaphor, the fact that poems can be free verse, and suggested they express their feelings in their poems. Paula's class all wrote rhyming poems:

FOOL

I remember when I was a fool
It was raining, I jumped in a pool
I wanted to be cool
I said "I will rule"
I remember when I was a fool.

YO MAMA'S DAY

Yo mama's day it's like a day for yo mama
Don't give her no drama
while you watch a cartoon orama
We got a new foster child Billy
So let yo mama enjoy her flowers and candy
And yo mothers day will be just dandy
Word up to yo mama
by Quincy

Elaine suggested they write quintains, which they had done before, and write about yoga, which ended up being rather successful:

Yoga

Happy, Funny
Jumping, Stretching, Blowing
Funny Elephant
Good Stuff
            By Yulisa Magdaleno

Yoga

Happy, magnificent
Screamed, balanced, stretched
Fun exercise
Animal poses
            by Jose Gastelum

The yoga poems were accompanied by illustrations that were masterfully executed, showing the different poses and animals associated with them. These little drawings are really inseparable from the poems.

By the sixth class in Billie's classroom, Yofe was already primed to teach poetry, and these students' poems are the best of the bunch. Yofe shared with me her approach to teaching writing as we sat on my back porch, and we agreed that I'd join her on her next run of classes to demonstrate a poetry class. As with classroom teachers, instruction in reading poems and discussing them comes easier to Yofe than thinking up writing assignments for the children. Non-writers of poetry tend to underestimate what children can do as writers, and end up with poems that are far less sophisticated than what children are capable of writing.

But the accumulated evidence of Yofe's reports on her preschool and elementary school classes convinces me that this artist has an eminently poetic sense as she describes class after class of teaching yoga. She suggested to Billie's class that they write about something they love or something they hate and describe it, using as many adjectives as they could to show what it looks like, feels like, smells like, tastes like...and if that didn't work, to become it and see how that felt and write about being the thing or emotion. It is not surprising that her students, who learn to do the poses by imagining that they are animals, can relate particularly well to the natural world in their poems:

OCEAN

I am the ocean blue and salty
I am the ocean rocky and wavy
I am the ocean watery and slippery
I am the ocean fun and hard
I am the ocean flooding
Water water on all
    by Militza

OCEAN

The ocean is blue
The ocean is green
Beautiful green turtle bodies
The ocean sounds like fish swimming
It tastes like potato chips.
    by Eman

I want to be a penguin
so dark like a shadow
the stomach, so light like a
cloud in the sun
they love swimming in water and fish
i am a penguin.
    by Francisco

It is, of course, not farfetched to link poetry to breath, movement, and poses. It seems that her students learned to relax and stretch by doing yoga and learned something about creating by listening to Yofe talk them through the poses. Certainly all the children benefited from the mental space in which yoga made possible different sorts of poems.

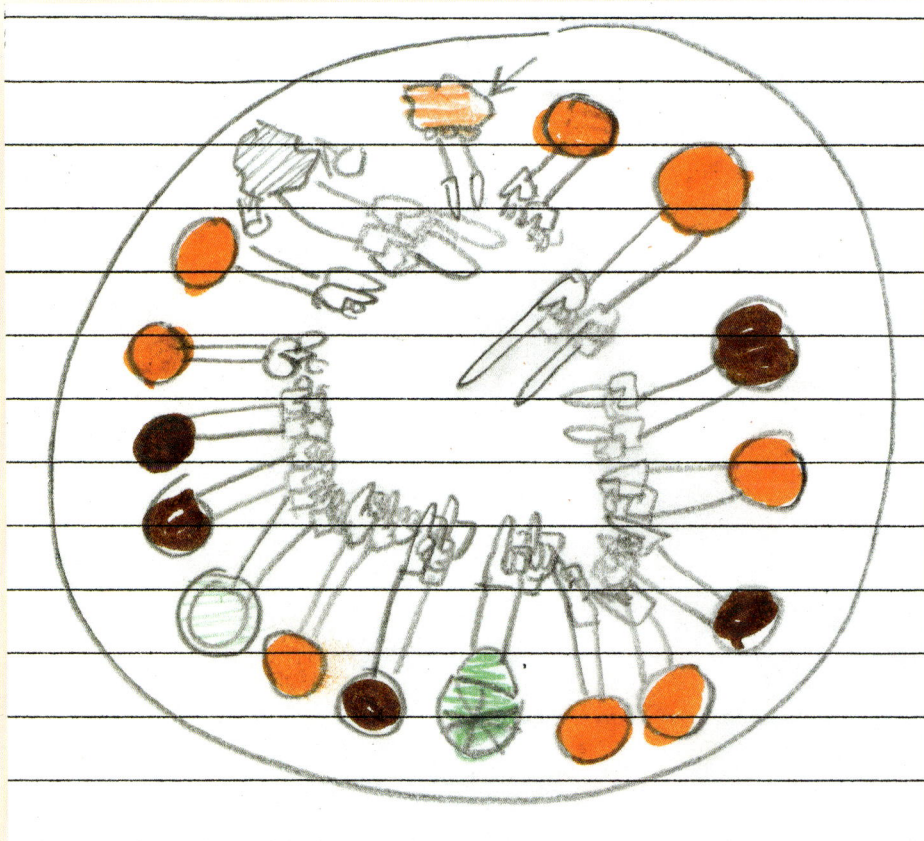

I am near
the water

and I see
myself in the
water

and on
top on the
water

I see
the sun
sparkling
in the water

Jorge

9
I feel very soft looking
at a sleeping dog

Coronado School is located in the heart of the Iron Triangle, the poorest and most violent section of Richmond, California. When you enter the school and walk down the main corridor that leads to the classroom, you are reminded of a jail. But when I entered the third grade classroom of Molly Salyk's class in the fall of 2007, an atmosphere of peace and contentment was apparent in the posture of every single child. They were all absorbed in reading a book, some lying on a rug, some sitting in their seats, no one speaking, no one looking up at me, a stranger, as I came in.

I discovered that this mood of safety, fostered by their marvelous teacher, Molly, who these children had had the good fortune to have for two years in a row, could not be disrupted. Even children who "acted out" in Molly's class never stopped looking to her for guidance and comfort. She is a young teacher who has learned the secret of fostering learning in the best possible way — she cares and manifests her caring in every word and gesture. I was also fortunate to be accepted into her classroom for a year to teach poetry.

This was my first experience of teaching poetry for several lessons in a row to nine-year-olds. These children who had come to expect a nurturing atmosphere at school, looked to me to unravel the puzzles and secrets of poetry. They all looked at me with eyes of such trust and openness that they at times moved me to tears. Molly orchestrated a little ritual each week: they'd sit on the rug, quiet and expectant, as we read a poem or a story together and discussed it. I was frequently surprised by the answers these children gave to my questions. There was one child who thought about the making of stories in such an original and sophisticated way that it does not seem like an exaggeration to say that he came up with his own narrative theory.

I made a practice of asking many questions and accepting all kinds of answers as I steered these children towards understanding a wide range of poems and a Grimms fairy tale. At times Molly jumped in to try to steer her students to the "right" answer that she thought I was driving at. But I came to believe in teaching these kids, many of whom struggled to read and write, by meeting them at the point of their openness. I gave them as free and broad a gamut of possibilities for responses as I could. Every class was a journey into the exploration of a poem or a story followed by writing something under the influence of what they had just read.

Frequently, they would not "get" my writing assignment, so then came the work that Molly expertly collaborated in of explaining to a nine-year-old how to fulfill the task with as much imagination as possible. I taught a poet who writes about the California wilderness. The students came to anticipate the next Pat Reed poem eagerly. With some trepidation, I then began to teach them about Picasso and the writer most closely allied with his experiments in abstract Cubism, Gertrude Stein. It was not so difficult really for them to understand my explanations of Picasso's paintings. I showed slides and pointed to what I was teaching them on the projection screen. But my presentation of Stein's most experimental poems, **Tender Buttons**, felt like a much more challenging kind of effort.

There was no picture I could point to when I discussed "A White Hunter," for example. I broke out into a sweat during one of these classes. I kept thinking, "how can I teach poems that are grammatically incorrect and make no sense to kids struggling to perform on tests that require correct grammar and a very narrow conception of how meaning is made?" But these children had no preconceived ideas about how they should write. They embraced Stein's poems as eagerly as Pat Reed's. And their writing started to show signs of original thinking, surprising juxtapositions, and more inventive writing.

Meeting these children where their minds opened in an atmosphere of kindness and peace became, for me, a weekly joy. I'm grateful to Molly and every single child in her class. Each one came over to me, each one wrote with all his/her attention and effort. Seldom has poetry been greeted with such seriousness and such pleasure. At the end of each class, many children would come up to read their poems. It was my work to respond to each child individually, to find the unique qualities in each poem.

Here are some of their wonderful, varied poems which formed part of a magazine that I assembled:

VANILLA

Vanilla is strong as the sun.
Sunny vanilla is not carrot.
Carrot vanilla is play station
Sunny is not vanilla carrot!
Vanilla: Vanilla makes me
think of lunchable.
                by Dajanae Thomas

WATER REFLECTION

I am near
the water
and I see
myself in the water
and on
top on the water
I see
the sun
sparkling
in the water
                by Jorge

Frogs
    and
rabbits
    hopping
        in
        a
        line
in
the
    forest
        by Charel

BARKING DOG

The dog is barking
at the sun because
It looks like a cat.
        by Jose

Take a scoop
of fun and
and take a creamy
sound like the
ocean waves!
        by Olanundra

THINGS

baby
fat
the
sun
my
room
chicken
and
rice
apartments
singing
play
ball
dead
bird cars
        by Charel

SLEEPING DOG

A dog that sleeping that is white
with black spots
I feel very soft by looking
at a sleeping dog a dog that was
barking a lot very loud
        by Jorge

THE SPARKLE LAKE

The lake is sparkle when it not mess
        by Nestor

THE BOWLING ALLEY

Come great ball of shining armor
Sparkle of the disco ball
All the people were in dark
black uniforms
In the colorful bowling alley there
was a big pretty palm tree that
was in the dark corner in the back
The corner was so messy
like a closet
So I fainted and didn't wake up
til seven o'clock at night.
        by Pepper

THE LAKE

blue
lake
to
swim
bright
sparkle.
  by Efrain

MALL STRAWBERRY

Mall strawberry is peas.
Red heads up is not lamp puppies.
Goldfish summer is cookie'n cream.
Cookie 'n cream is not a lamp.
Strawberry is puppies.
Puppies is not peas.
Lamp is peas.
Mall is not a lamp.
Goldfish is a puppy.
  by Alia

CAMOUFLAGING FROG

The frog sparkle blue
running around camouflaging
different kind of blue
like the sky.
  by Tyrone

MY CRAZY THINGS

Sunny is gorilla apple
bed is not Home Town Buffet
she is pickles cookies Chocolate
she is not Red tag
  by Nestor

THE STRANGE MOUNTAIN LION

Its fur is fluffy like a rug
The mountain lion is yellow
The fluffy mountain lion is shedding
He makes a sound for prey
He loves it
The sound is loud
From the distance
I see something coming
The distance is no more
The lion looks at me strange
It's moving through trees
It's coming faster
He bumps into a tree
I run away.
  by Pepper

10
No answer was wrong

The fourth grade class I taught at Grant School in San Pablo in late spring of 2008 was notable for the shocking written accounts of accidents and murders the children saw in their neighborhoods. I decided to present three lyric poems I wrote immediately following the death of my brother. His death, which was a suicide, caused me immense pain for I lost the person in the world whom I loved the most. It also caused me to write the best poems I'd ever written. Given this coincidence of suffering and poetry, I thought it would be a good idea for me to share some of my poems with these ten year olds.

In the first two sessions, I focused on a couple of poems about the homeless by the San Francisco poet, Sarah Menefee. Typically, I give my students a copy of the poem, and then I present numerous questions about it, designed to help them think about it. We discuss the meanings of individual words and phrases that might be difficult for them to understand, and look at the ways the poet conveys those meanings, in Sarah's case through the large spaces she uses to separate individual lines and the ways she creates images and sounds.

For instance, look at the two poems to the left:

u can't describe his homeless eyes in the sunburned face

ere everything has been destroyed but the human sadness

ze of dignity deeper even than anger and rage

t's deepest somehow out there busted down to the pavement

erything else is ashes

I taught these poems on two successive days. With the first poem, probably the first "real" poem these students had ever encountered, I started with very simple questions: What do you know about this man? Does the poet tell us anything? How does she tell us? Does she use a positive or a negative statement? We spent some time on the question, why is there a space between the two lines of the poem?, and what is the effect of so much space? I also asked them, Why is this poem so short? Is it enough? Would it be a better poem if it were longer?

My "method" for teaching poems, adult sophisticated poems, is to ask many questions, essentially creating and leading the discussion through the answers, multiple answers, my students give in response. And there were many responses, and in that first class I turned no answer away. No answer was wrong, and if it was somewhat out in left field, I'd interpret it in such a way as to bring it back. The students who talked that day, and the ones who didn't, sat up straighter and looked more involved as they saw that there were no wrong answers.

During the next class I taught the second poem, and this time I did let them know that some of the answers weren't really answering the question. But by now they seemed ready to learn more about how to talk about a poem. I felt my way, sensing an opening in their interest, a receptivity to participate in the discussion in multiple ways, but to steer closer to the meanings in the poem.

The first question I asked about Sarah's second poem was about the meaning of "blaze of dignity." I separated the words in the phrase and we first focused on the meaning of "blaze" and secondly on the meaning of "dignity." It was difficult for them to put together the two words and uncover the new meaning. But when I asked where the blaze of dignity was "deepest," they knew right away where "busted down to the pavement" was. We next talked about the choice of the verb "busted down" and why she used that expression.

So, already students were learning that the words in a poem are chosen for a reason. In the first poem we discussed how the poet says she cannot describe homelessness for she refuses to attempt to describe "his homeless eyes;" and yet, she arrives at the burned out "human sadness" even more powerfully since everything else is wrecked. The writing task I gave them was to describe a homeless person, focusing on a part of the face or body or clothing to express an emotion.

My students had many recollections of homeless people they'd seen in the streets, some of whom turned out to be relatives of theirs. I was alerted to the intelligence of one child, whose name was Edwin, who used the word "overwhelmed" in a discussion of one of the poems. But I found him and the boy next to him giggling and horsing around during the time allotted for writing poems. I went up to them and said, "You boys must be feeling a lot of pain about something and that's why you're laughing instead of writing."

The child whose vocabulary had impressed me wrote a few lines. He read them to me. They described a murder he had witnessed the week before. I had asked the kids to write about something "bad" that led to something "good." Sarah's poem arrives at a place so burned out that everything is ashes, and in that awful place, the deepest thing is revealed as that "blaze of dignity." The imagery of blaze is linked paradoxically to the final image of "ashes," as though the dignity is so "ablaze" that it burns even as it redeems.

We wrestled with the paradoxical complexity of this very short poem and talked at length about the idea that the capacity for dignity could "somehow" be deeper than the "anger and rage" a homeless person would justifiably feel. Several of the students described a homeless person and moralized that, in spite of the fact that he was homeless, he was glad to be alive. But Edwin just narrated the murder he'd seen without supplying any redeeming outcomes. I didn't ask for any. It was enough that he was able to withstand the fear and pain of writing it down on paper.

Thomas Prather, the teacher whose class I was teaching, commented after the second class that ten children had participated in the discussion of Sarah's poems. He predicted that all the children would talk soon. What neither of us anticipated was that every single child would write poems in the third class.

After leading a discussion of my poems about my brother's death in the third class and giving them a poetry writing assignment, I hung back and didn't move around the classroom to talk individually with children who needed my help. I sensed something new in my experience — that these kids would now write very well on their own. And I was right.

What got these kids writing? I wasn't sure if it was the topic of my poems — the death of a relative — or the fact that I was now teaching poems I'd written. This is what I gave them:

NOT OF THIS WORLD

III

Not of this world
your vision
you bent
towards the mountains
you scaled
that broke
you
and severed you
from me

IV

My heart is chill
Ice lodges in your place
dissolving into grief
I melt and shiver

I asked them, what do we know about the person addressed? What happened to him? What does it mean to scale mountains? What is the meaning of "severed"? How can someone's vision lead to the ending of a relationship? What does the poet/speaker feel? What is happening to her heart? Where is the place of the dead person? What does he become? In this way, we charted a course through the metaphors of a "vision" that scales mountains, a heart that "dissolves" into "grief," and a loved one who is displaced by "ice." It was a painstaking process as we passed through these steps to grasping the nature of the relationship; and it was thrilling, for these kids jumped into the poems with a new intensity.

Next, I prepared them for my writing assignment. I asked them, has someone you know died? How did you feel? How did that person die? Write a poem that describes someone who died. Describe yourself, your feelings. What are you like now? Did you change at all? Who did you become?

These questions opened up an arena familiar to all these children that they were more than ready to write about. Wendy had an instinctive grasp of writing succinct, short poems that epitomized her feelings:

> *you died and left*
> *a sadness in me. I*
> *miss you so grandpa.*

I became aware of another child, Leleni, at the end of this class who had a different relation to writing poems than anyone else in the class. She approached me and handed me several pages written in an indecipherable script without smiling, silently indicating I should read them. I spent several minutes attempting to read her large, scrawling hand, but couldn't. I took the pages home and, with the aid of strong reading glasses, was able to type most of it up. Here it is:

My great grandma died
when I was only
three years old.
She used to play
with me
and plant gardens
decorate them
and we used to have
so much fun.
The day she died
was in 2004
When I came over
Mom dropped me off
and she went to work
I knocked on
her door
and it was open
I called her name
and I didn't hear
her everything
was broken.
Glass was on the floor
the water was running
and I turned it off
I went to her room
and she was lying

on her bed. I touched
her – she was cold
and hard like someone
stuffed and then I knew
she was dead
I lay beside her
When my mom came
to pick me up, everything was
on the floor
and she called me
and when my mom
came in the room, she saw
my great grandma
and me lying
next to each other
and she said,
"What happened?
What did you do?"

I said, "I didn't do anything.
When I got here,
she was like this.
The cops said

they were on their way."
and I started to cry
in my mom's arms.
I felt like my head
was about to explode
and my mom said
everything was going to be
as I said to her
no it's not
and I love
my grandma
so much
and I still wish
she was here
I also still think
of her
right now.

From that class onward, Leleni continued to write pages and pages of poetry. She seemed to be the one child who took very seriously the act of writing, identified with it, and found in it her own private vehicle for expressing her thoughts. When I read this poem aloud to the class a couple of weeks later, a hush settled in the classroom as they listened to this child's story of the death of someone who was important to her, a death she could not accept.

In an earlier classroom, two years ago, I had been at Washington School with Diane Sullivan's fourth grade class. Michaelle Goerlitz, a drummer, was visiting with Diane's students the same year. Marie Josee, a Latino child, was handing me poem after poem, folded up neatly in small packets with hearts drawn on them. One of her poems went like this:

> *sometimes is magic*
> *I can't see his eyes but*
> *darkness to a light*
> *I know where I am*
> *going I know you are*

A year later I went to see Diane to ask her some questions. The Johnson Foundation had insisted that I come up with some statistics about how VALA artists had changed test scores. Diane was blunt. She couldn't give me any statistics for, she went on to explain, she refused to try to "measure deep learning." When I continued to press her for results, she mentioned Marie Josee as an example of a student who had been a non-reader and a non-writer before Michaelle and I came to her class to teach. With music and poetry, this girl had turned into both a reader and a writer. She was not the only one.

But Diane kept the resounding outcome for the end of our conversation. As a result of her exposure to VALA artists, she had changed her way of teaching writing to her students. She no longer taught "to the test." She told me that she'd started to teach by genre and remained open to whatever her students chose to write about. Diane had effectively revolutionized her teaching of literature and writing.

Half of Diane's students were Latino, and half were African-American. Thomas' kids are all Latino, and it is a big challenge for most of them to write and for some of them to write at all. During the next class, many of them were eager to read their poems and when one little girl began to read her poem, I expostulated, shocked, in the middle of her reading when she revealed that her aunt had accidentally run over her own child.

Poem after poem uncovered the terrible realities these young children carry in their minds. Two of the children informed me at the end that they hadn't read their poem to the class because it was "too personal." I said to one of them, "It's good you wrote a poem. It's not like a newspaper that everybody can read. Very few people read poetry."

I am aware that I am creating a culture of talking about, writing, and reading poetry for children who have never before encountered it. They are learning that poems can be the site of expressing their most hidden and difficult feelings. Gradually they uncover what is locked away and keeping them from speaking and writing. It has also become my opportunity for facing things about their lives in an intimate process of exchange.

By not writing about themselves in school, I'm convinced they are blocked from learning to write much at all. I've seen that the writing they do with me leads some of them to come to writing just as Marie Josee and others do.

The first time I talked about something that was important to me personally, my students started to talk among themselves. I spoke quietly in a tone that did not command attention. I told them that I had realized recently that really terrible experiences can be the spawning ground for some of our best experience. It was at the close of the hour. I felt a little uncomfortable and wondered why they chose to stop listening right when I was telling them some profound information about myself.

Now I know why. When they have strong reactions to what I say or what I ask them to write, they cope by diverting their attention from it. At no other point in the class had they turned away from me. They were capable of flawless attention. So now I know when they are most deeply affected — it is when I enter into an aspect of life that is "too personal" to speak of in front of the class. I was out in the open, speaking of a realization I had and it was scary for them.

I only needed to call them on it quietly from time to time and continue opening up possibilities for poetry so it would be OK to hang out there in that drab classroom in a space where they would feel free to hear my words and their words just among ourselves.

I like a eagle
to fly in the

11
You could actually hear the children listening

Today, more than ever before, children were calling out, "Ms. Rotenberg! Ms. Rotenberg!" What had I done to unleash this volley of voices? And all at once? I'd felt freer today as I was teaching Mr. Prather's fourth grade class about line breaks and chosen three of their poems as examples. Was it that I'd typed out their work instead of the work of poets they'd never heard of? So today I felt confident as their teacher, confident that they'd "get" what I was trying to teach them about how you break lines one way and not another way. I wasn't testing the waters with them anymore. I'd gotten to a point where I knew them. I guess I must have felt that they accepted me.

Daniel called me over to his desk and I was explaining to him how to break the lines of his poem, but he didn't understand it. So I read his poem out loud and asked him to listen for the pauses. Then I left him to give a vigorous explanation to another student. They all wanted to know if they'd gotten it right. They were all clamoring; and I was with Daniel again, and I did something I never do — I made pencil marks on his paper. And at last his poem was right, and he must have felt freer too, because he started to talk. He told me that the monster in his nightmare was still there and wouldn't go away, even when it was day time and he was awake. He told me that he knew he "imagined" this, but then he forgot that and the monster was right there, very real. I said calmly and quietly, "but you know, don't you, that it's your imagination." He looked at me with wide intense eyes, probing mine, and insisted the monster was there. This is the poem he wrote:

My nightmare
is my terror and strife
is next to me in my
thoughts and in my
life all I want is for
them to go away now
and forever.

The way these children start to talk is something I'd already seen in the previous class. A little girl began to tell us about the death of a relative. She talked on and on for about thirty seconds. Then another child raised his hand and spoke some. Then the same girl raised her hand and talked some more, picking up where she'd left off as if there'd been no interruption. The whole class listened. She talked rather softly from the last row in the class. You could actually hear the children listening. Her story continued on and off for most of the class. It was almost as though she spoke for all of them. It was the only time that very few children raised their hands to say something. When it came time to write, the kids wrote poems that exceeded all their previous efforts.

Wendy is able to put her feelings into a poem with succinctness and power. Nevertheless, this matter of the line breaks escaped her too. I thought she was extra smart. I couldn't understand why she wasn't grasping it. Perhaps I hadn't spent long enough explaining how to make Alfredo's poem more effective. I had not noticed Alfredo before I put up his poem on the board and asked, "Who wrote this poem?" Alfredo raised his hand with a big embarrassed grin where he sat at the back of the class. Like many of the other children his poem narrated a death, a murder. I'd asked the kids to talk about how they felt, and many of them seemed to know just how to "say" their feelings by simply telling how things happened. Here is Alfredo's poem, after we edited the line breaks:

My nephew died
from a mistake
'cause a cop shot him
because they confused him
with the robber
so when he reached
into his pocket
they thought he had a gun
so they shot him
he then handcuffed him and
when he tried to get up
the cop shot him again

he was trying
to reach his legs
and they thought
he had a gun
so they shot him
and killed him
and he was only
12 years old
and I didn't even
meet him
I didn't even
see a picture.

Maybe we were all excited today — me, for my reasons, and them, because we'd already come so far in writing about terror and suffering, and today we would just deal with line breaks. And we would even break up Bre'Asia's poem about her grampa getting sick with cancer and his lungs falling out just before he died running on his way to the door.

Only Edwin had almost got the line breaks perfectly the first time he handed his poem in. I told him he had a good sense of language and asked him whether he'd read poetry before. I was having an adult conversation with him, for Edwin was a child with an adult soul, even an adult way of talking. He was proud of his skill. I'd chosen his poem first, even though it was the last one placed on the page I handed round. It went like this:

I got out of the freeway
there was a homeless man.

His clothes were ripped his face was burned
He was saying out loud "Homeless need food please."

I asked the class to tell me about Edwin's homeless man. They selected all of the details except for the "burned face." As usual, these students remained quiet about the part of the poem that was both the most frightening and the most mysterious. When pressed, one child offered that he might have been "burned by the sun." That comment let the rest of them off easy. These kids, who regularly observed homeless people and murders in their neighborhoods, lived with nightmares that visited them at night and haunted them by day; for the monsters regularly perched on their desks, and were written into their notebooks; and who could convince Daniel that the bite felt on his shoulder was not hurting him long after he woke up?

I regularly passed the children playing kick ball on the asphalt playground outside their portable classroom. It looked a little like a moonscape — grey, hard, hot — with children screwing up their eyes as they poised to kick the ball.

One morning on my way to their classroom, I noticed Daniel standing by himself, squinting at nothing. I smiled at him and said, "hello." He didn't even see me. Was he the only one out there who entertained monsters regularly on that arid asphalt in the open, alone?

12
It's a secret inside me

For my final class with the fourth grade students at Grant School, I brought in an excerpt from a prose poem I was writing. Mr. Prather usually spent a few moments calming the students down, telling them to stop eating popcorn, take out their writing books, and put away everything else. This time he also mentioned that this was their last class with me and quietly added that he'd learned as much as they had from these classes with me. It was the most graceful way for a classroom teacher to thank me that I'd ever heard and I felt pleased.

So I read the piece I'd Xeroxed, and looked up at them from time to time, to see if it grabbed them. I'd brought in a poem by a favorite American poet of mine, John Wieners, the week before, and they'd talked to one another and refused to follow along or listen as I read "A poem for record players." I'd decided that the poem wasn't up their alley. But this excerpt, which began as follows, seemed to speak to them:

We listened to the sounds as they came from the kitchen.

Each child listens.

I brought a coffin of no hope and we sang from terror.

Before the trouble came, we were children; but the winds from the north are grim.

We harbor tales of dying in our mouths.

I'd heard from my students about their "tales of dying," and I've already written about the way they opened up and spoke of this when the other children and myself and Mr. Prather listened.

In my piece, I wrote about a people who had stories to tell that were riveting, but their audience was disappearing. They wandered listlessly, while memories troubled their minds. They lost their mothers and their fathers. I asked my students, "What does it take to write something down? If it is too private to tell, what happens if you write it out, just for yourself? What happens to a story when you put it in writing? What happens to us when we write? If you tell it to someone, is it still private? Why might you want to tell a secret?"

All these questions about telling and writing addressed issues relevant to this class in which most of the children told stories and wrote poems for the first time. I want to record the letters and poems written in this last class, at least the ones that were handed to me, that weren't too private to be seen, and the ones that were private and still passed on to me, because they were meant for me.

Israel, who had never handed me anything before, thanked me in a letter for teaching them poetry for six weeks, concluding with "you're a nice poet and your poems are awesome and cool." How terrific that Israel liked the poems I brought in, and seemed to attribute them all to me! Cynthia, a hitherto unnoticed child, thanked me for teaching them "how to write poetry and how to read it the right way." Certainly we had spent a lot of time discussing the poems I brought in to read, but this class had grasped many "right" ways of reading poetry, almost from the start, and I had just guided them as they led me. Then Maria, who had rebelled against participating in my class, almost until the end, wrote down exactly how she felt:

I don't want to write because I am tired
& I've had a rough year. And also because
I'll miss all my teachers in my life.

There were a few children, who'd been writing poems all along, who handed me poems, not letters addressed to me. Bre'Asia, who spoke so quietly that I always had to ask her to repeat what she said, transformed her experience in this poem by attributing it to a boy:

this boy hurting inside
trying to figure out
*   why why he had*
to scream fight
*   kick and punch*
*   punch right in the*
*   face writing this*
poem Just for someone's
*   love someone to love him*

Her ability as a poet was already apparent from her poem from the week before. She was one of the few kids who'd been inspired by the sounds Wieners catalogued in his poem. She wrote:

> *The wind shifting from*
> *the north, birds chirping*
> *singing a song, crickets at*
> *   night going crikit, crikit, crikit*
> *the natural nature sounds*
> *   don't break*
> *apart*
>
> *The pipes of a*
> *motorcycle and*
> *   when you're drilling something*
> *in the wall, the sound of*
> *a crash or an explosion*
> *   goes boom boom*
> *   hear the sounds of something*
> *hand made*

Or Wendy, who had been handing me short simple poems about her feelings since the first class, gave me a poem describing an imaginary scenario:

> *Naked in the sea dying*
> *of hunger meters away*
> *can't get to shore because*
> *he can't swim.*

Bre'Asia and Wendy's shifts into a fantasy realm were new for a class that had pretty much stuck to a rendition of their own experience. A door had opened for both of them after we talked about ways of writing that hid us from view.

Edwin changed the meaning of poems that were "too private" to a poem that was only meant for me:

"It's only for you!"
Sometimes I like flowers
But I hate things with flour
It's a secret inside me
Although I can't say we
I could tell it to you
'cause it's the right person too.
But your hair looks in the mood
I feel like you're good
I don't know if I'm immense
But I can sure climb a fence
I am not real attractive
But I'm sure really active.

I thought many of these students seemed bright, but Edwin was the brightest. He'd answer my questions with subtle, complex thoughts and language. "It teaches things that you never knew that you knew" was a response he gave to a question I asked about how a poem reveals things. My poetry class had given these kids a way to talk about themselves; and by talking about what they saw and felt, they found a way to arrive at writing, and even a way to occlude themselves by writing poems.

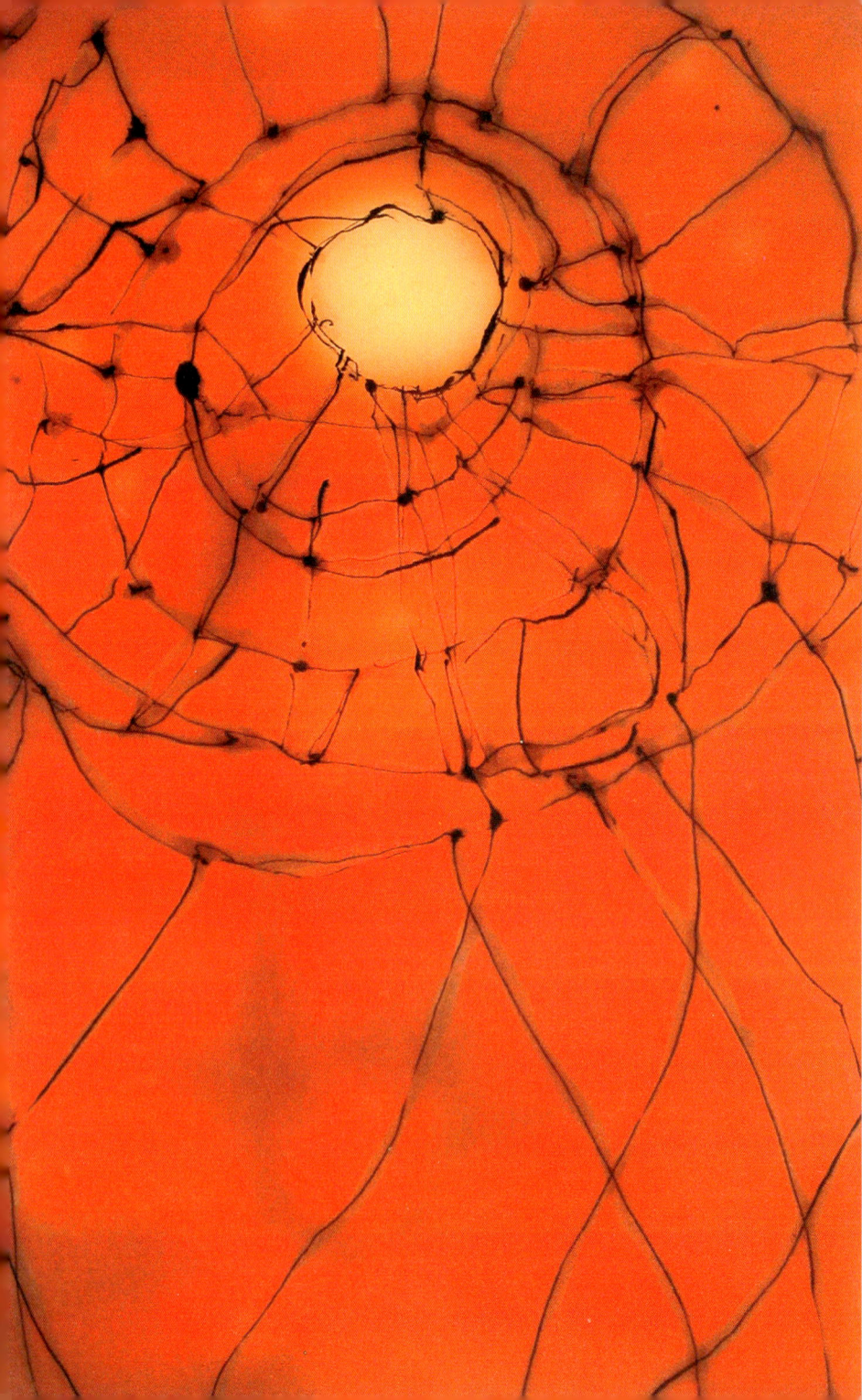

13
Why did you bother to come to teach us?

Augusta Talbot, an earnest, initially shy woman, came to VALA through the recommendation of the painter, Amy Trachtenberg. This painter, who could get children to do the most impressive and beautiful artwork, passed on the torch of her inspiration to Augusta.

I spent Augusta's entire first residency in the kindergarten class at Nystrom School, observing and coaching her. Augusta, who had not taught such young children in a long time, was hesitant at first. But from the beginning, I was impressed by her seriousness. She'd prepare for each class extensively, often spending many hours, even late into the night on her projects for the following day. No artist before or since has spent as much thought and time as Augusta in this way. And it paid off.

She worked with the theme of "Wind" from the Open Court Reading literacy curriculum, mandated by the district of West Contra Costa. This curriculum tends to be unimaginative and irrelevant to the lives of the African-American and Hispanic students in this district. But artists like Augusta imaginatively invest it with exciting, creative possibilities. She brought in a script she adapted from a story about the wind for her students to act out with shadow puppets she taught them to make for a theater she put together late into the night before she brought it to the classroom for them to perform in.

osite page:
usta Talbot's encaustic,
de of bee's wax, mounted
lexiglass.

97

Something I recognize in hindsight was that Augusta was very adept at quietly making a meaningful connection to the classroom teacher. For that matter, her emotional sensitivity enabled her to establish strong relationships with her students in this first class and in each subsequent class she taught for VALA.

The next year, in the fall of 2005, I assigned Augusta to two preschool classes. I think she was somewhat taken aback that I gave her the youngest group of students we had. But she quickly adapted to the needs and abilities of this population and proved herself as gifted a teacher of three-and four-year-olds as she had been of kindergarten aged kids. She invented her own ways of reaching them artistically. She taught two classes at King School in Richmond to make dinosaur masks by using books about dinosaurs as research tools and reading material. She asked them many questions about dinosaurs and then taught them to draw a T-Rex, an Ankylosaursus, and a Triceratop, words that they learned in the process of making their masks. Then they paraded around the school with their masks, which became famous in the West Contra Costa preschool office.

In the spring semester, she told stories from three books about snakes to these same children. The children listened to a story she made up about snakes and their families, and she then taught them to draw a snake that they painted. She created the alphabet, as the children instructed her, by drawing the snake's body into shapes of the letters. Afterwards they colored in the letters with bright markers. Finally, they painted black lines around the letters. The teachers strung the letters together like prayer shawls and hung them in the classroom. This project marked a definite step forwards in Augusta's use of story-telling and art-making to teach children to create the alphabet joyfully and with a sense of interest. In preschools, where one of our goals was teaching the students to learn how to write and to recognize letters, Augusta was one of the only artists who successfully accomplished this.

At Washington School preschool class, Augusta read the children *The Little Engine that Could*, and discussed trains with them. Each child painted a character that Augusta cut out and pasted on boxes that they also painted. Each child was then fitted with a box as if it were a train car. Here is an example of a cutout painting:

In the spring semester, her reading of a story about the life cycle of frogs turned into a discussion in incredible detail of the passage from baby eggs to adult frogs with her three- and four-year-old students, many of whom spoke English as a second language. From live drawings that she drew, the children painted a tadpole and a pollywog, and later drew their own frogs.

Augusta also listened to and recorded a story that one of her students told her about dinosaurs. She then used the story to make a shadow puppet show with the story as the script. The children drew their own puppets and Augusta cut them out and made them the characters for a performance that the children did with a theater that she built. Her projects turned out to be both challenging for her and tailored more and more closely to the capacities of her young students. So Augusta turned out to be a masterful teacher of preschool students, demonstrating that a very fine artist can call up her own creative powers to invent artistic projects for children of any age.

Augusta went on to teach third grade at Washington School. She helped children come to an understanding of paintings from Picasso's pink and blue periods, some of which were represented in the literacy curriculum under the theme of "Imagination," and she introduced them to Gertrude Stein, whose importance in Picasso's life she emphasized by reading to them from a biography of the painter. Here are some of the paintings from this class:

The intensity of the colors in these students' paintings reminds me of the vibrancy of the color in some of Augusta's work:

This past year, Augusta went on to work with the same theme of "Imagination" with two grade three classes at Cesar Chavez in Richmond and two grade four classes at Wilson in San Pablo. She added the artists, Romar Bearden and Daniel Elton, who did photography and made collages using cut up photographs, painted pieces of paper, and paint. There is a rigorous logic in the progression from last year's work with Washington third grade students through the third and fourth grade students this year, as she carefully and conscientiously built new projects on the previous ones.

On the first day, she gave each child two pieces of paper and instructed them to paint in different colors of pre mixed blues, patterns which she demonstrated on the board. This is how the classroom of blue patterns looked at the end:

One of the things Augusta emphasized was that her demonstration was there to get them going — it was not something they should try to copy precisely. Augusta laments, "In spite of this, almost every child in all four of the classes in both schools were sure they were 'messing up.'" But she continues, "They were very anxious and resistant until they realized I really did want them to see what came as they worked. One striking thing to see was how different each child's painting was from the others; how unique each child's marks were." In my experience, this is the sign of a good art teacher.

There was no difficulty persuading Augusta, who reads a lot of poetry on her own, to let me come to one of her classes at Cesar Chavez to teach poetry. It was a love affair for me to bring in a poem by Langston Hughes, who had been a friend of Romar Bearden, to teach Augusta as well as the classroom teacher, Miss Pricemant, and her third grade students to write poetry. All of them were eager, emotionally open, and clearly prepared by Augusta's presence to welcome a VALA artist into their midst.

Augusta introduces this context very well: "Cesar Chavez is a beautiful school. My impression of it is that the teachers are very engaged with the students and that there is a lot of parent participation in school activities. All but maybe three of my students were Latinos. Both Miss Diaz and Miss Priceman felt that they wanted the children to understand something more about self-expression, taking creative risks and using the imagination. Because of the rigorous testing requirements, these teachers have no time to do hands on art projects."

She continues, "My first class was in Miss Diaz' room. She was very enthusiastic and willing to help in any way I needed. So were the children. I have never met such a thoughtful and helpful group of third graders. They volunteered to pass things out, pick things up, wash the paintbrushes, sort everything, and even move

my materials into the other classroom. If we called on the girls to help wash, the boys would complain that we weren't giving them a chance to help!!"

Miss Pricement was also thrilled to have an artist come to her. She was practically in tears as she explained that the lack of time to teach art made her job much harder. She feels that art offers something to the children that they desperately need. Here are some examples of their students' artwork:

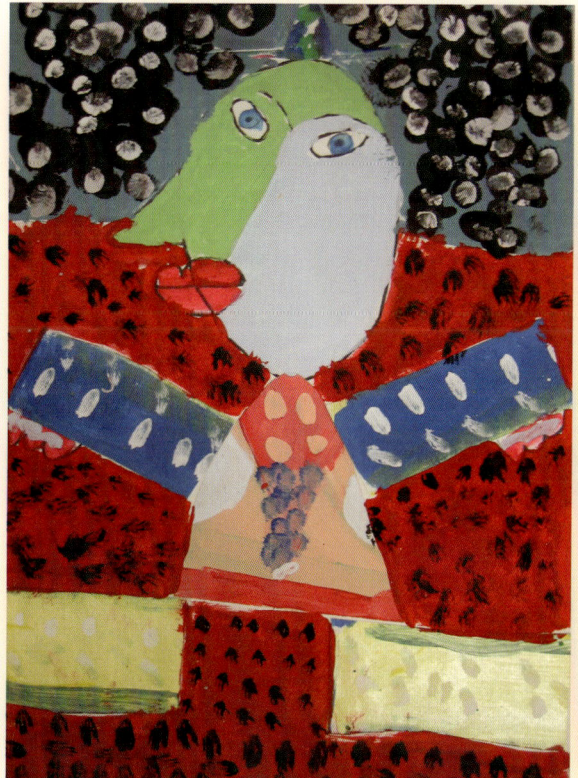

When I came to this class to teach poetry, I taught a Langston Hughes poem. I'm giving the full text of the poem to show how the students repeated some of its words, lines, and images, and used the principle of repetition with variation in Hughes' poem, so effectively.

As I Grew Older

It was a long time ago.
I have almost forgotten my dream.
But it was there then,
In front of me,
Bright like a sun –
My dream.

And then the wall rose,
Rose slowly,
Slowly,
Between me and my dream.
Rose slowly, slowly,
Dimming,
Hiding,
The light of my dream.
Rose until it touched the sky –
The wall.

Shadow.
I am black.

I am down in the shadow.
No longer the light of my dream before me,
Above me.
Only the thick wall.
Only the shadow.

My hands!
My dark hands!
Break through the wall!
Find my dream!
Help me to shatter this darkness,
To smash this night,
To break this shadow
Into a thousand lights of sun,
Into a thousand whirling dreams
Of sun!

I asked them thematic questions such as, "What does he compare his dream to? What do you think his dream is?" and "What does the wall do? How is the poet connected to the wall?" and "Where does he lie down? What happens to his dream?" I also showed them how the rhythm builds through the repetition of words, and the meaning of the lines comes with the variation in the repetition. We focused a lot on the final stanza and how there is a transformation in the oppositional relation between sun and shadow at the end of the poem. I tried to show them that Hughes breaks the shadow into a myriad of dreams of light. It was difficult for them to grasp this idea, though, in focusing so closely on the poem and how it is built, they heard its language and rhythms very well and transposed them into their poems.

I asked them to identify their dream and their shadow, to think about a memory that expressed who they are, and write about something in their experience that reminded them of the poet's dream of light and wall of shadow. This is what they wrote:

Bad Dreams

It was a long time ago.
I have almost forgotten my dream.
My father went away for a year.
I had a nightmare everyday that
something was wrong.
I was scared something happened
to my father
Since my father had left I had night mares.
There I saw the shadow…I told
the shadow, leave, leave,
you're not welcome here.
You don't know how it feels dreaming
about your father it ever trouble
Later that year my father came
the shadow never came back.
> *by Stephanie*

My Very Bad Dream

It was a long time ago
I was a little girl
I dream of a bad dream
I was sleeping
I dream of a doll jump
at me.

I woke up I told my mom
and I sleep with her I feel much better
No more bad Dreams for me.
> *by Maria*

My Dream

My dream is
to see my
grandma and grandpa.

There is wall between me
I want to break
it but I think
I can't

I say I want to
break this wall
and I can
my grandma
and grandpa.
                    by Anayancy

Sunny and Darkness

It was the day after tomorrow
I was dreaming a good dream
then the darkness came.
It blocked the light of my dream

Every day a little bit of light
Came in me. But every day
darkness came in me.

DARKNESS!
DARKNESS!

I am afraid
I wish it would
Just go away.

I hide under
my bed thinking
it would just
go away

Go away Darkness!

Please Go Away!

The night before that d[
the darkness went awa[

For just thinking a drear[
a better dream
the darkness went awa[

I was happy
really happy
which was good.
really good

The darkness
never came
back it went
away

Thankyou!
For going away.
                    by Judith

My Dream

It was a long time ago
My mother died
I dreamed that she was
with my dad all the time
Only if you were with me
Only if I could see you
My dream
My dream
My dream is to be
with you. My dream is
always to be next to you. I wish
you were here with me. But I'm
happy
                by Claudia

Last Night

I dreamed a sad dream.
That my grampa died.
Just in front of me.
There I was right in front of him.
A guy shot him.
Just just right in front of me.
I ran and ran to my grandma's house.
I told her about my grandpa.
Then I told my mom too.
And then my dream went away
because my grandma said to dream…
of a happy thing.
                by Nayel

Augusta's photographs of the artwork done by her students at Wilson School and her narration of teaching there are compelling: "Wilson Elementary was a much more difficult place for me. Both teachers, Mr. Thompson and Mr. Leung, were great. They each have thirty-three fourth graders in their undersized classrooms. Some of the children are seriously troubled and cause the teachers endless problems. Both teachers wanted me to do the same thing I had done at Cesar Chavez. I taught collage but also some basic principles for drawing self-portraits. Each child then made a bound journal-like six-page book. Attached to the front page was a black and white photograph of the student. The following spread had a poem by the child on one side and a drawn self-portrait on the facing page. On the remaining two pages they wrote more or did comic art. The books are beautiful, incredibly creative, and in many cases, very personal." Here are some photographs of her students' work:

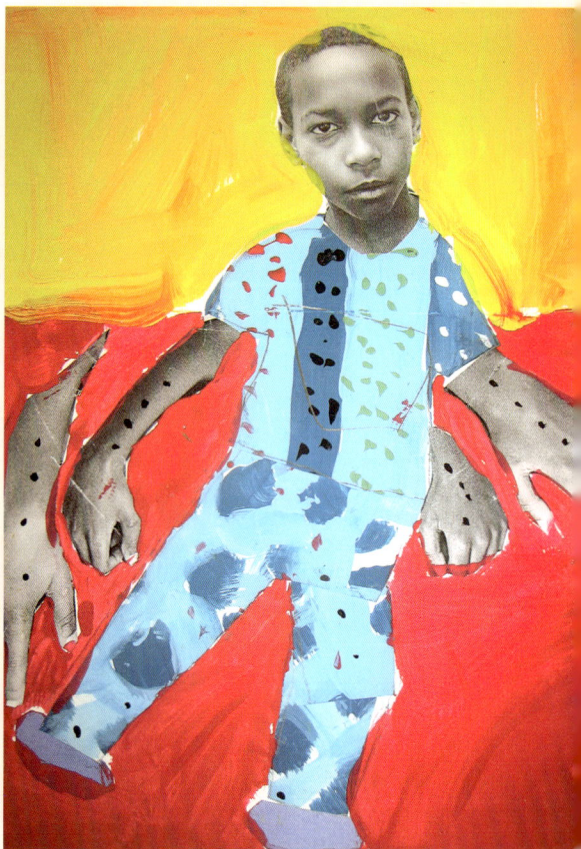

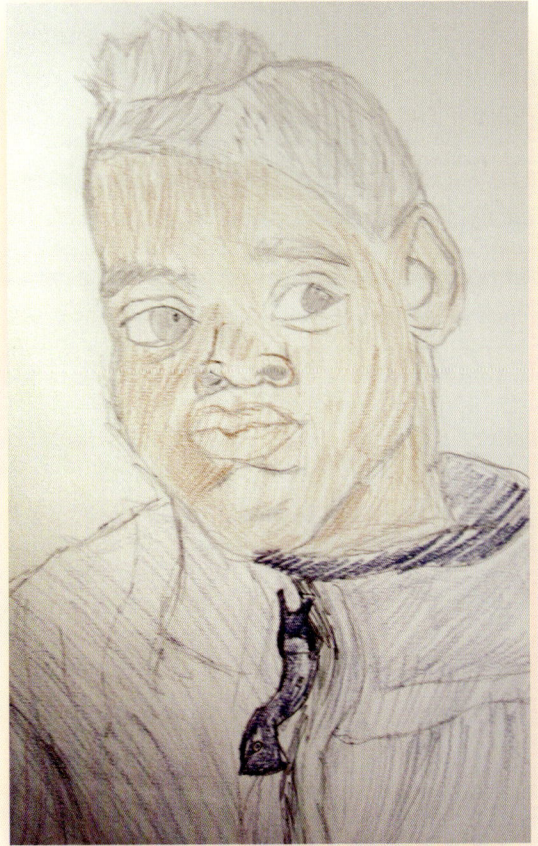

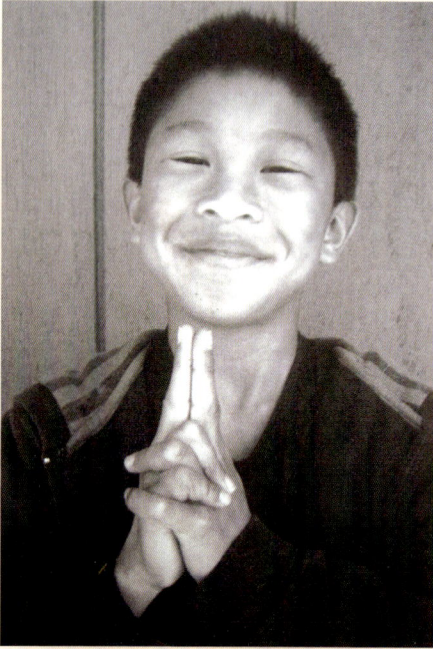

Augusta begins this latest report of her teaching in a memorable way: "On the last day of the last class I was teaching at Wilson elementary School in Richmond, I 'interviewed' the fourth grade students. I asked if the art classes had taught them anything, and if so, what. All but one child said they loved having me there. Some said they learned that they could draw in a way they never dreamed possible. Some said they learned how to mix paint; others said they loved not having so many rules all the time and that it was cool not to feel like they were always messing up.

But Julius, — the student who is the most disruptive the teacher has known in his entire teaching career, who sits apart from the others, who has violent out breaks and 'family problems' — said it was a waste of time. When at the end of my interview I asked the class if they had any questions for me, Julius raised his hand and asked why I had bothered to come to teach them."

Augusta took this question very seriously, and her report is an attempt to answer the question she feels she didn't have the presence of mind to answer adequately at the time. Her answer — in the report I have been presenting — is not really a revelation to me, but it is, too. It is not so much the words Augusta uses to present her reasons for teaching these kids, as the passion that comes through when she says them, that is notable. Her involvement with these children who, in her words, "have experienced a lot of sadness, separation, violence, poverty and abuse," is intense. Let me quote Augusta's imagined response to Julius' question: "Making art is not a silly past time: It is a form of self-expression that can save your life and save your soul. While making art, whether it is dance, singing, poetry, painting, film, or something else, it is possible to express your worst fears, anxieties, rage, worries, and also your greatest love and thrills." She continues, "For most of you, it may not become what you do to make a living; but learning how to creatively express yourselves will, I promise, help you make sense of the confusing and sometimes violent world we live in."

I only mean to point out that, whereas a great teacher existed in the substratum of Augusta's being, her true colors as a teacher of these children emerged in the spring semester. I don't attribute this full-flowering to my momentary appearance in her classroom, but I think a conversation in which I insisted that Augusta commit herself to this teaching for a full year contributed somewhat to her putting herself wholeheartedly into it.

When Augusta told the two teachers at Cesar Chavez that she would probably be returning to their classrooms next fall, they were happy to hear it, but worried about the other teachers who already were feeling miffed that they had not been selected to have a guest artist in their classroom.

Because of Augusta's ability to get close to the teachers in whose classrooms she teaches, she is the VALA artist who is the most receptive to hearing their feelings about her teaching as well as learning about the dissatisfactions of those teachers who didn't get her. And because she was particularly uncomfortable with this recurrent phenomenon (it came to her attention last year as well), I decided to take action and bring it to the attention of the principal. The need other teachers were expressing somewhat vociferously for VALA artists at Cesar Chavez became part of a movement of approaching all the principals in West Contra Costa where VALA had a presence to get more funding and more classes for VALA. And it worked!

Not only had the principal at Cesar Chavez school heard from his teachers, but principals at Wilson and Grant were also finding out about the successes of VALA artists. The principal at Wilson School, Sonja Neeley-Johnson, a particularly memorable woman who seems to be up-to-date on what is going on at her school minute to minute, was the first one I met with, and she agreed to double the classes and triple the funding support at her school. She also mandated that Augusta and I would come in twice in the fall and twice in the spring to do teacher-training workshops in painting and poetry! After Sonja stepped up to the plate, the principals at the other two schools where we had started working in the spring of 2008, were prepared to match her. It became a historic time for VALA, and I thank Augusta for initiating all this momentum.

At the same time as this was happening, I was taking a series of workshops for Executive Directors at the nonprofit training center, Compasspoint. I was somewhat leery of the possible value of a course titled, "Thriving as an Executive Director;" however, in spite of the fact that the new-age language of the two leaders should have been designed to put off any self-respecting poet, I found the sessions valuable. No session proved to be more valuable than the one when we wrote the names of possible supporters on cards and I was asked to select the person best suited to advise me now. Imagine my surprise when the card I selected turned out to be my own father whom I informed copiously about my work, but had never set up an appointment to consult him about issues related to the running of my nonprofit. His own expertise culled from managing his own business and sitting on the boards of countless nonprofits proved to be invaluable. Within a short span of about ten minutes, he learned enough to advise me to disband my Advisory Board and create a whole new board!

So this is where VALA stands now. I'm pulling together a new board of people whom I want to join me in the work of carrying on a rejuvenated VALA. West Contra Costa, where VALA has been practically the only arts organization serving public schools, has suddenly made available a lot of money for the professional development of teachers, which VALA aspires to do by showing teachers how to teach children the arts and creative writing in consonance with the literacy curriculum. VALA artists are, one by one, learning to teach poetry in addition to all the other arts. And I have just hired five new VALA artists to fill the slots made available in schools in

Richmond and San Pablo, dramatically increasing our artist pool. It is a very hopeful and exciting time. We are managing to eke out a place for the arts in the lives of children between the very narrow slots left after the testing that teachers are forced to do. We are hearing from teachers more and more that they need us. They remember what it was like when they could teach their lessons creatively. I'm going to conclude this chapter with a very eloquent letter from a young teacher of a third grade class at Washington School, addressed to the principals in West Contra Costa.

I showed up in Graciela Lechon's classroom this past spring, 2008, to teach poetry for Ayodele, an African-American Congolese dancer. There was no other artist as quick or as eager as Ayodele to absorb my poetry lessons. But this time it was not the children who captured my attention, or my concern for instructing Ayodele, but a highly intelligent classroom teacher. When I was delighted by the ready creativity of her students, and praised Graciela, she started to cry, and said, "I teach phonics, just phonics, day in and day out, and I know how creative my students are." She was terribly afraid that she was squelching this creativity and the tears streamed down her face when I told her that somehow she was managing to teach in a way that clearly did not squelch their creativity. She begged me to offer arts workshops for teachers that summer. When I prepared to meet with principals, she offered to write a letter. It goes as follows:

Dear Listener,

A few weeks ago Tina facilitated a poetry exercise with my students. I wish you had been present. There were no special props, just the reading of a poem, Tina's casual and brief analysis, and a captivated audience of third grade students. It all came at me like a flash flood in a desert dry wash: the years of creative writing and literary analysis, the engaging discussions, the children's enthusiasm—all the beauty and grace that teaching **once was** for me. The rise of scripted teaching has erased all that. The art of teaching has been replaced with the dispensing of decontextualized, mechanized, isolated facts. Children are assumed to be empty vessels awaiting our direction rather than eager, creative flames to be fanned.

I cannot overstate my emotional reaction to the lesson Tina presented. My students were like butterflies emerging from a cocoon. Their creative spirits were burst forth from the weight of the Blue section, Green section and ill-advised Red section. They thrilled in the outcome of the beautiful poetry that blossomed from their thoughts.

We desperately need the influence of artists in our classrooms. We have moved so far in the extreme direction that I foresee a generation of illiteracy. But, not like the illiteracy of past generations in which people could not read. This is a new illiteracy: that of a generation of people who cannot think, ponder, philosophize, imagine, critique, create.

We need to access programs such as VALA and to expand their role to be something similar to the role of a curriculum guide. We need time to collaborate with artists as well as on-going professional development in arts integration and the teaching of Art as a discipline.

The time to re-direct our focus is now.

Thank you,

Graciela Lechon
20 Year Veteran Teacher

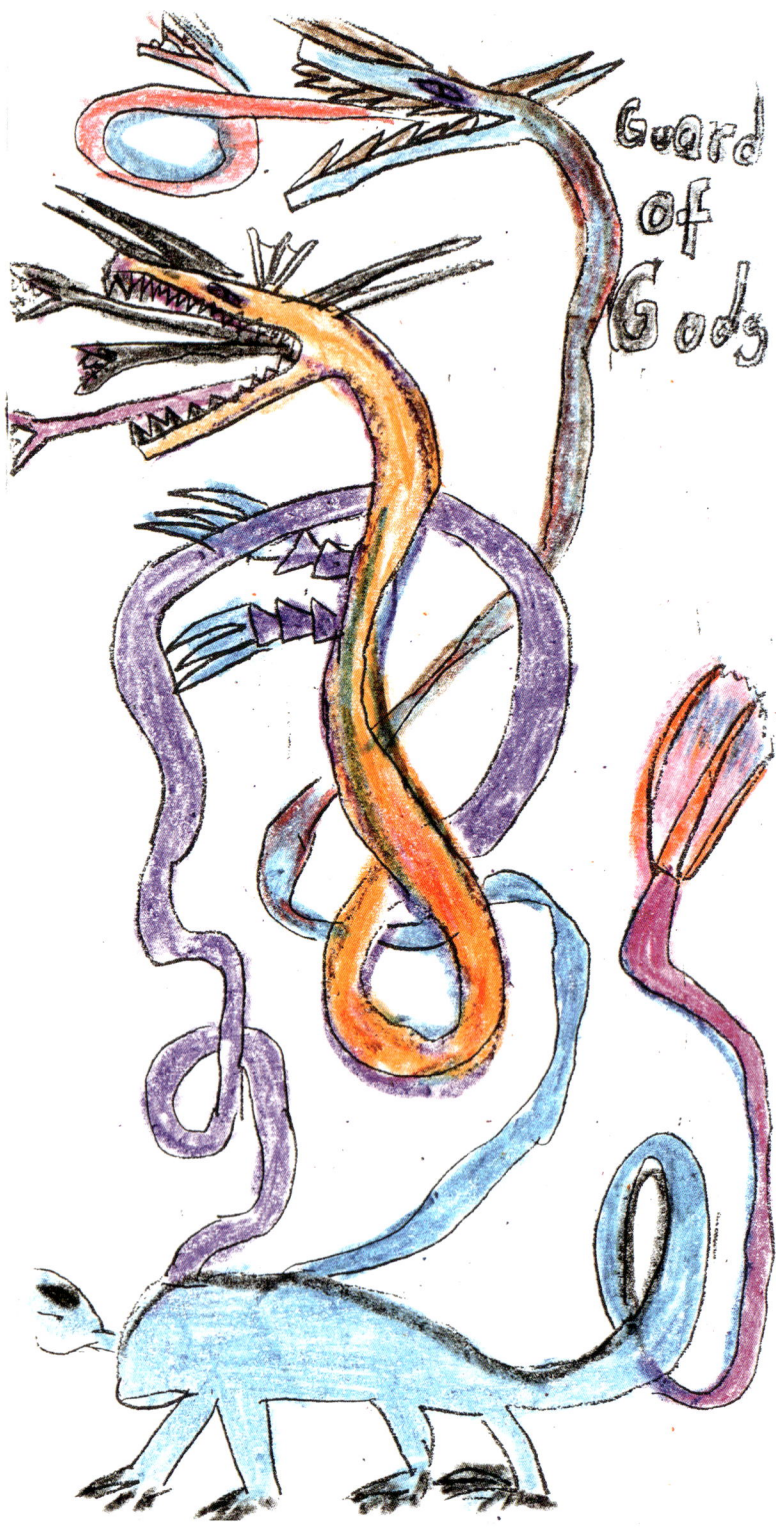

Guard of Gods

14
The Furtive Devotion of a Forgotten Generation

There's nothing quite like working with a VALA artist who is a writer. And there is no one more gifted at combining the visual arts with language than Alastair Johnston, *enfant terrible,* and brilliant Scotsman. He would repeatedly infuriate me with his disregard of my authority, my rules, even my requests; but when he picked me up to take me to see his classes, whether they were at Cragmont School in Berkeley six years ago or Washington in Richmond Point a year ago, he'd show me a side of him I came to value — this was the Alastair who could take twenty nine-year-olds patiently through the fourteen steps he'd conceived for them to make — a what? — a "lotus book," folded in multiple folds and shaped like a lotus flower. Teachers were in awe of this guy, children adored him, and who would wonder why? This blustery, critical, rebellious man turned into the gentlest of teachers once he crossed the threshold of the classroom.

Alastair repeatedly reminded me, in the most direct and unabashed fashion, that rules were there to be broken, and that approaches to teaching the arts were only as good as the artist was a thinker, a creator, a human being.

His reports are frequently witty, wry, with a keen sense of the ludicrous that he brings to bear upon problem children, projects kids can't do, days when the classroom teacher is absent and mayhem ensues. But his tightly-packed narratives mostly convey, in the end, how hard he works to transmit complex book projects and imaginative mythic literature to children who seldom come close to receiving such richness from any other source.

Here's a description of a favorite self-portraiture book project from his most recent report:

> "Weeks two and three were involved with the class portrait, where I take a photo of the kids and cut it in half. They then complete the picture and write a bit about themselves. This went well and they all got into copying my block lettering and Tuscan from the blackboard. There were two problem boys in Mr. Royce's class, Erin who is slow, and Gerry who is perhaps backward as he kept saying he couldn't do it and basically I had to do his work for him. I later figured out he is a lazy kid who just doesn't want to do anything. I think he has emotional problems too as he is a bully, but he cannot focus and wanders about pestering the others. They wanted to learn blackletter but I was a bit rusty."

And it's not only in the classroom that Alastair tirelessly exerted himself:

> " To get the books ready for the next week, I scanned them all and tweaked them in Photoshop and then laid them out in InDesign and in the end just printed the books out on my computer & inkjet printer to save time, though it took me about 8 hours to do this. Certainly a lot more than I had calculated. The biggest waste of time was trying to print multiple copies from my computer: first I backed up the wrong sheet, then after I reprinted those I found my printer was feeding two sheets at a time, so again I was getting the wrong pictures on the backs. So I wasted time and paper till I got it right. I also printed the covers."

Without pause, he concludes his narration of the creation of the portrait books:

> "The third week was just a matter of folding and gluing and it went well, and then they personalized their accordion books and I photographed them showing them off."

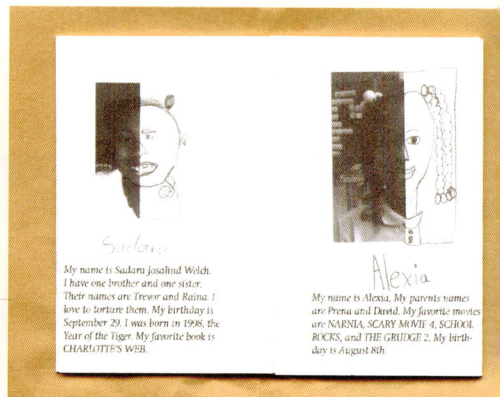

My name is Sadani Josalind Welch. I have one brother and one sister. Their names are Trevor and Raina. I love to torture them. My birthday is September 29. I was born in 1998, the Year of the Tiger. My favorite book is CHARLOTTE'S WEB.

My name is Alexia. My parents names are Prena and David. My favorite movies are NARNIA, SCARY MOVIE 4, SCHOOL ROCKS, and THE GRUDGE 2. My birthday is August 8th.

Alastair's evaluation of his classes at Grant School read a little like a jam- packed adventure story. This is what happens when a new project is paired with a substitute teacher:

Week four was my first bad day at school. Ms. Hoopaugh-Jones called to postpone the class a day so I went at 10:30 for Mr. Royce's class. Mr. Royce was also out and there was a substitute teacher, Ms. Cherry who sat at the desk and let me get on with it... Before I read them the Native American stories I talked a bit about the Native Americans and their lifestyle, particularly here in the Bay Area. One kid, Gerry, who is a pain, said he did not like African Americans. Since Cherry is black this was a pointedly rude remark, so I told him even if he felt that way he should not express it, and I tried to talk a bit about toleration. I also said there was a difference between Native Americans and African Americans, but he does not listen. Then I started talking about creation myths and one kid said, "Read the Bible, that's all you should do." So I had to detour to talk about different belief systems without getting too blatant (I am an atheist and am personally opposed to ALL organized religions, however I do not talk about this in elementary classrooms. Furthermore like most atheists I have studied the Bible closely and have the ammunition to argue against ANY christian belief, but this was not the place to browbeat a 9 year old.) Suddenly a siren went off, it was 11 o'clock and the kids were all jumping up saying it's a fire. No it is not a fire, I said, Then it's an earthquake! said one kid and dove under his desk. It took a while to calm them down. Ms. Cherry went out and came back and said it was nothing. The reading went well; then I explained how the animals had human attributes and they should pick an animal, then write and illustrate a little story. Then things fell apart. Gerry made a paper airplane and threw it away. Then he took another kid's paper and crumpled it up. Finally he and Omar went off to a table in the corner and drew spiders. When I went over to quieten them down and try to coax them to work, they cursed me in Spanish. I pretended not to understand, but then when one of them asked me a question in Spanish I replied in Spanish. Most of the kids worked but there was so much hubbub and problems I had a hard time coping. They started singing "Itsy bitsy spider" in unison, which was fine, but then they got rowdy and I had to tell them to stop singing and get to work. They couldn't focus. Many wanted individual guidance or more paper, or had not been listening. Mostly they had no clue how to write something from their imagination, so it was a struggle for the whole period...."

This artist is as focused on teaching the complex book projects to fourth graders as roping in difficult children, whom he rails against, but you get the feeling after a while that he cares about them as much or even more than the successful students whose good behavior he mostly leaves out of his report.

The most recent portrait book Alastair handed me is slight, compact, masterfully executed. Each piece of writing is a haunting, moving variation on the last. I can imagine the children pestering Alastair, "What should I write?" and him saying, "What does anyone write about?... your favorite food, your favorite color, your name, your friends' names...." And then the brilliance of the assignment comes up in the repetitions and the minor tremulous variations in the repetitions from child to child. Then when some writing stands out, it really stands out, but then again, only in little ways. Take, for example, Kristienelle:

> "I am from Guam. I like bananas and apples. I have a dog named Noggy and a cat named Catty. My favorite book is JUNIE B. JONES. My favorite food is a big chocolate cake. My favorite colors are pink, blue and red. My birthday is October 29. I was born in the Year of the Tiger."

Kristienelle

I forgot to say that this particular version of the ever-recurring portrait book is a foldout book in miniature and all the writing is carefully typed beneath each child's portrait — half-photo, half-child's drawing. Each child gets his or her own copy. Even I get a copy when Alastair manages to salvage one from the great demand for them in the classroom.

It's the middle of the night and Alastair's book projects call to me but I can barely see around me and I now see that the portrait book I just quoted from is from a book from last year at Washington School, or was that the year before last? I stumble to my little bookshelf where I keep Alastair's kids' books and can't find the one from this year. Who cares? I don't turn on the light. I pick up what I think is the star-shaped book which Alastair recently borrowed to copy and then brought back. But it's the lotus book I thought I lost, and I open one section of the lotus and it's a story of a god who was a demon (and this guy claims to be an atheist!) I always thought Alastair wrote the lines on this book, but the letters are somewhat sloppy. How could anything sloppy be Alastair's??

So this is what comes of writing this Vala book at 3:00 in the morning.

It's close to 5:00 AM and I can now see my Alastair shelf. I've found his book, *My SOLAR System*, and the portrait books made this past semester. Mr. Royce's class looks out at me like portraits from the future — haunting, beautiful, sexy, funny, hidden. Each hand makes him or her into whomever they are.

Their voices are various, but, for me, "Militza Marquez" comes to my attention as, yes, a joyful Hispanic ten year old:

"I want people to know that I like helping my mom and I like to do my home work. I like playing sunpiece because we can play with friends and have fun a lot to play. Just like me."

In her portrait, the joy that radiates is quiet, gentle, expansive. Her own drawing brings Alastair's half-portrait photo into the light, extending it, emphasizing it, making it more prominent. In this way teacher and student interact and enhance each other's vision.

Alastair's last day with the teachers' classes seems like the most perfect effort:

"Week 6 was devoted to a single book, an origami flower book…. First I had them come up with things associated with winter: weather, birds, plants, animals, holiday events. I made a list on the board. We talked about evergreen trees, migratory birds, whether Santa exists or not. I tried to explain the concept that if he did not exist it would be necessary to invent him (as Voltaire said of God). Reindeer, mistletoe, holly & ivy. I said if two people meet under mistletoe they have to kiss. What if it's two guys? asked one of the boys. It's up to them, I replied. They got bogged down in the transcription to the special paper I had brought, then the folding was a problem also. In the end we didn't get far enough and as Ms. H was making one too, I showed her how to do it and then during the break I helped half a dozen of the kids finish their book, so they could show the others. There are always one or two who get it and want to volunteer to help the others, so it works out. It was cold outside too so I went straight to Mr. Royce's class and we started. His kids were on best behavior, some boys had made paper "spinners" for me and three or four girls had written me letters of appreciation. We used a timer to complete each part of the exercise so they had ten minutes to write, ten minutes to transcribe and revise, and so on. Again the folding proved complicated. Say it in English, one of them said sarcastically. Gerry floated about doing nothing and basically being a nuisance. He kept asking to sharpen his pencil, till there was no pencil left. It's a simple book but the tricky fold stumped a lot of them, though I took it slowly and tried to demonstrate it clearly, so again I went around and helped the half dozen hopeless ones. Some had gone ahead and encountered problems, so I had to get them all to sit down and I explained the next step and told them to go no further. However Mr. Royce was making one too and he was able to finish his and then help the kids around him. One of the girls Joanna, who *is very quiet, got it right away and ran around showing others the trick of the flower fold. We finished in good time, so then Mr. R had them talk about what they had learned from me over the 6 weeks, and again expressed a desire I would come back in spring."*

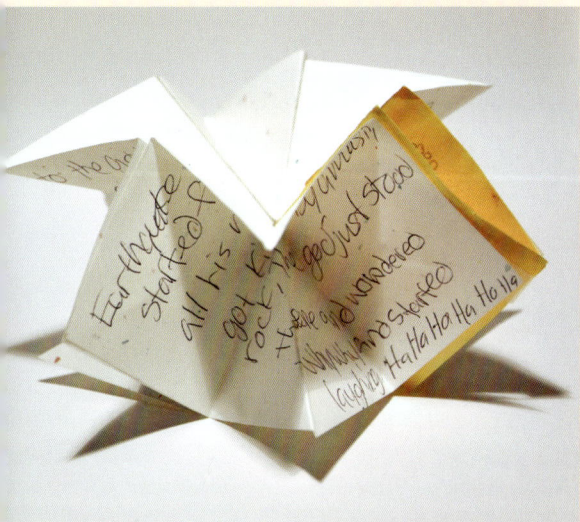

Does it sound a little like assembly-line style of book making, or does it perhaps more resemble the furtive devotion of a forgotten generation, composing and writing down and even making their own books?

So Alastair's whiz-like rendition of this process really hides a devotee passing on his art, his passion, and the disappearing skills of reading, writing, drawing, and building ever new and renewable book structures.

I'm concluding this book with this artist whose inner confidence, nested within a cantankerous exterior, distinguishes the artist who has worked the longest for VALA.

I feel surrounded by these artists, these children we teach, in an ever widening circle that's also catching teachers and principals in its trajectory.

If we remain true to the arts we practice and teach, children and their teachers will find us and join us in a celebratory passage of discovery. I believe in the power of this teaching, this exchange of gifts between artists and children, children and teachers, and artists and teachers. The power and the love of the arts and poetry kindles a flame of hope and vitality wherever we bring it.

Creative Inventory
I

As funding started to come in, artists of all different disciplines came to my attention, each in their own surprising way. Until recently, I never had to advertise for artists. I did not believe in canvassing art schools, keeping costs low by paying art students a minimal fee. The artists who have come to me have been top-caliber, sometimes internationally renowned, frequently recognized in the Bay Area cultural community as the best artists around. I always believed I could train a really good artist to work with children, even without teaching experience, through a mixture of verbal instruction, assistance, and collaboration, and it proved to be true.

I met the first artist who worked with me on a visit to New York City. I was passing a café and recognized someone inside. I went in to say hello, and fell into conversation with the woman my friend was talking to, who turned out to be an actress and director from San Francisco. She had a grant from the California Arts Council to do theater with kids and, when she learned that I was writing stories for children for my programs, she proposed that she hire me to make theatrical pieces out of my stories. When her funding fell through, I promptly hired her to work with me.

At John Muir School in Berkeley, our first site, there was a fourth grade teacher who had previously taught kindergarten for years and had landed the most unruly class in the school. He begged us to come into his class. We decided to take these kids on, and I remember that when Sheila announced that they were going to write a script for the story I'd read to them, there was a howl of protest. After fifty-five minutes, I told them it was time for them to stop writing their scripts, and there was an equally vociferous howl of protest!

Sheila Balter, who now tours France regularly doing her own spoken word productions, went on to teach several other classes with me and other artists. She was also the first to do professional development workshops with me for VALA. She was always recognized as the one with the most energy, the one who was the most fun. Years after VALA was founded, it was not difficult for me to choose Sheila for our tenth anniversary celebration as the artist who had contributed the most. Her combination of commitment to the children and the teachers, engagement with her own art, and high spirits were an inspiration and made her one of the many partners-in-artists I needed to build a unique organization.

One musician I'll never forget is India Cooke, internationally renowned jazz violinist. I walked into my house one morning to find my husband interviewing a marvelous looking black woman. She looked straight at me and asked me what I did. When I told her, she flatly informed me that she wanted to work for me, even though she had no experience teaching children. I was delighted. But India was more than I bargained for. When I told her what her fee would be, after a lively exchange of jokes and information, she said, "Let's take a ride in my old MG to the nearest café and talk." At the café, India suddenly shifted from being a charming conversationalist to a hard-nosed businesswoman. I can't remember now if she insisted I double her fee or merely raise it by seventy-five dollars. I pleaded with her that VALA's meager funds could not accommodate such a hike, and furthermore, if I raised her fee so astronomically, I'd have to raise all the other artists' fees. She said, "Raise their fees. They'll appreciate it." And they did. Through this negotiation, India assured that no outstanding Bay Area artist would balk at joining VALA's artist pool.

The other piece of information that India laid on the table when I informed her that every VALA artist must write a comprehensive evaluation of their classes before they'd get paid, was that she couldn't write, she couldn't type, she would only dictate. Little could I know that those dictations would floor me as she narrated the extraordinary things she did in residency after residency. VALA's required writing exercises became musical notations of the most creative sorts. Instrument making became the raw materials for creating orchestras. One classroom teacher was the narrator of her students' story about landing in a spaceship in Hawaii as the animals that stepped out of this spaceship turned into the sounds that filled the classroom.

You could well imagine that I wondered, what next? I invited India to participate in one of our first teacher training workshops in Richmond. What I learned then was that this exquisite and powerful violinist could plan, write, and type as well as she played. Susan Wittinberg, Director of the West Contra Costa Educational Fund, who hired me to put together a crew of artists, singled out India for praise for the way she'd planned and written her description of her part of the workshop. Susan told the rest of us to model our written presentations on India's!

There are several other musicians that affected my life, my work, and my practice as an artist. None more than Glenn Spearman, who arrived in San Francisco with his saxophone and electrified the jazz scene. His charismatic personality charmed the hearts of VALA's children with an inimitable musician's ease of humor and love. I paid him an embarrassingly low fee, early in the days of KMAWP, to teach the history of the Harlem Renaissance and play with an unmistakably sweet series of jazz melodies of his own while I (or his music) got the children to paint. One third grade student, Armando, actually painted a facsimile of Glenn's saxophone. Other children painted from their imaginations. Everyone loved it — just as much as Glenn did. He taught me that music was the key art for kids.

I also remember with an acute sense of shame that I offered Glenn a meager fifteen dollars to play as the introductory number for a children's poetry reading at the Berkeley Art Center. He did not like to stand and wait, though it was almost impossible for me to predict when the endless classrooms of kids would finish presenting their work and reach our kids. So Glenn did stand and wait, but when he played, it was like a sound from heaven descending upon us all.

Some time after that event, I invited him to meet me so I could offer him another class. He looked uncharacteristically thin and frail and admitted to feeling sick for a while. It turned out he didn't have the money to spend on medical care, so he had gone the route of alternative medicine. I was worried, but proceeded with my agenda and invited him to teach again. When I told him the fee, he looked pained and conflicted. He turned me down. I offered him two classes and he accepted. Then I had one of my most remarkable experiences with any VALA artist. I had been drawing portraits for years and asked if I could draw him. We got on the subject of my drawings and I admitted to having a portfolio of about forty portraits of children I'd drawn when I was studying art and working in an open classroom school in Cambridge, Massachusetts. Glenn wanted to see them all. So I opened the portfolio case, which had been closed for years, and we put children's faces all over the living room and dining room floors. Glenn walked around them all, entranced. If I hadn't already "fallen" for his music, I fell for this human being who loved children so much, he could really see each one looking at him from my drawings. He promised to make a date for a portrait drawing.

There have been two tragedies during my tenure as VALA's director. The first for me was when I learned Glenn had colon cancer and then he died two weeks later. I was in L.A. when I was called about the funeral date. I changed the date of my return flight, flew home, and walked into a funeral parlor to hear some wonderful music accompanying Glenn's soul somewhere close to everyone there.

There must be a torch handed on from a dead musician to a living one. At the funeral, one of his friends played the sarangi, a classical Indian instrument. I approached him as he was sitting in the back behind the building and boldly asked him, "Do you ever work with children?" He nodded and I requested his phone number. Kash Killion proved to be as sparing with words as Glenn was fluent, but he knew how to teach; and collaborating with him as an artist and a poet in a second grade class at Malcolm X was unusual only in the way I've come to discover the capacities of children most recently.

In his first three classes, Kash taught his students exactly what the sarangi was made of, how it was built, how sound was made with it, etc. Step by rigorous step, he brought them to the point of playing it. Then, dressed in ceremonial Indian garb, he sat on a sacred mat, and played for easily distracted second graders for an hour and a half. I asked them to take out their pencils and draw him as he played. Kash's focus, seriousness, and concentration must have flowed musically into these kids, for each one drew continuously one single drawing while he played. The drawings were complex, detailed, not like anything I'd ever seen by second graders, let alone by older kids.

In the final class, I taught them *ragas* from a dog-eared book that Kash had loaned to me. My assignment for the children was to choose two words and make them part of a poem of their own. Here are some examples from the ragas:

BHAIRAVA

Upholding Ganga, the crescent moon upon his brow, three-eyed, wrapped in the skin of an elephant and adorned with snakes, his scarf white, his garland of human skulls, armed with a burning trident — so triumphs Bhairava, the first of raga-s.

BHAIRAVA

His limbs smeared with ashes (that lovely body), his brow lustrous with the cool rays of the moon, trident in hand and mounted on a bull, such is Bhairava, and so the sages tell.

You might think that the ornate language and syntax would be beyond eight-year-old children, and yet the richness of the words transmitted to the children's poems a sophistication and beauty that was very uncharacteristic of the typical writing of second graders. But I'm sure that it wasn't just the ancient Indian prayers that informed their work, but the deep exposure to Indian music that Kash's expert instruction gave them.

I had started this organization with an assumption about the interconnectedness of the arts, based on my own experience as a poet of frequently drawing and painting when I wrote. Collaborating with artists like Glenn and Kash showed me first-hand how potent music was as the tissue that tied together all the arts.

II

Two Native American artists I hired were particularly notable both as teachers and as people. Debora Iyall, who was a visual artist and a musician, was introduced to me as the Program Director at the American Indian Contemporary Art Gallery in downtown San Francisco. VALA was extremely fortunate to get access to AICA the way we did during the last two years of its existence when it inhabited a large space near Market Street in downtown San Francisco. AICA was an important center for Native American art, culture, and history.

Debora excelled as an art teacher and was also one of the first artists connected with VALA to teach poetry in conjunction with the visual arts. In fact, when I went into one of her classes to demonstrate the practice of poetry to her and her students, the class didn't seem to see me. They saw only Debora. It might not seem obvious to the observer what exactly catches the attention of young children. After sitting with Debora's class, it became clear. This woman who might have struck you as basically nondescript held the key to her students' hearts — she really cared for them; and they knew it.

Debora's first program focused on a show on exhibit at AICA about the California Gold Rush. At that time, VALA artists were still free to make use of the social studies and science curricula of each teacher. Later she also taught a program on an exhibit of Kabote's paintings shown at AICA. Jenine Antoine, the director of the gallery, continued the life of the center on-line after it lost its space during the internet boom when the cost of space increased three-fold. When this catastrophe occurred, we also lost Debora, since she could not afford to continue living in the Bay Area after she lost her job at AICA.

A second Native American painter showed up one day some time after I emailed Jenine begging her to recommend some Native American artists. Sean Nash was actually part Native American and part African-American. He was outstanding in his ability to communicate with kids; but he had no sense of how to negotiate his way in a classroom with the teacher. So for this reason, and because he didn't have a car, traveling everywhere by skateboard, I'd drive him up the hill to Cragmont School, watch him teach, mediate his relations with the teacher, and drive him down. He came on skateboard to my house with his backpack full of paintings, and taught the children Native American sign language, history, politics, and art. He taught them to draw and paint Native American iconography and did it brilliantly. He never talked down to the kids, and he conveyed complicated sophisticated ideas to them, captivating them as well as the teacher.

I'll never forget the day this friendly, outgoing, seemingly joyful artist turned to me and confided that he was murderously angry. I learned as much from him about what it was like to be Native American in that sitting as I did when he regaled his students with lesson after lesson of Mayan, Aztec, and North West American Indian history.

He frequently did auctions for VALA, selling his paintings for far less than they were worth, and giving us the proceeds. He showed at the Oakland Museum, the Mission Cultural Center, and sold his paintings to passersby on the streets of the Mission in San Francisco. Now hc is a professor of film and art history at California College of Art and Laney College, and was recently invited to the Sundance Film Festival as well as Cannes to show an animation film he made. So this rebellious, kid-like, utterly generous artist has become a success; and yet, when I asked him to come back to VALA again recently, both as an artist and an Advisory Board member, he immediately agreed. He still talks a mile-a-minute, sounds just as idealistic as ever about teaching art to kids, and really, he's my kind of artist.